Global Gender Reflections: Progress or Regress

Barbara Wejnert
University of Buffalo

Kendall Hunt
publishing company

Cover image courtesy of Jolanta W. Lieb

Kendall Hunt
publishing company

www.kendallhunt.com
Send all inquiries to:
4050 Westmark Drive
Dubuque, IA 52004-1840

Contents

Preface

When Cold War politics lost as the organizing principle behind international politics, development became the most import policy goal of every country and international organization. An underside (and a human side) to development exists, and feminism has made advances into the highly technical debates and ambitious predictions of examining what the future really holds for the people who will live it.

Women live dangerously throughout their life as far as safety, lack of rights, and undervalued social position is concerned. Empowerment of women is therefore critically needed if the future world is to be prosperous. Women empowerment, however, could be achieved only if there is a shift in perception regarding women's worth with an adequate understanding of socio-cultural and economic status of woman. The broad array of concerns related to women include issues of cultural stereotyping of their societal roles, problems of globally spread violence again women, working conditions and income capacities, protection of health, education, and representation of women in politics, professional, and top managerial positions. Thus, a holistic approach should be taken to understand women's needs and the challenges that they face every day.

Gender within Global Development highlights the ways in which feminist analysis has contributed to a richer understanding of international development and globalization. Combining theoretical, empirical, and political perspectives, the book includes cutting-edge debates on development, globalization, economic restructuring, global health, and feminist theory.

The manuscript attempts to answer several questions pertaining the contemporary situation of women in a global world. Among these concerns are: Does global development alleviate feminization of poverty or contribute to it? Has free trade hurt women (especially poor women) more than helped women? What are globalization's effects on women rights and education? Does global development bring women together or harm their closeness?

This book is dedicated to academics and practitioners studying and practicing in the field of gender and global development. At the same time, the book is also the ultimate primer on global perspective and gender, appropriate to use in courses in a variety of disciplines addressing gender and contemporary development issues both globally and within the United States' context. This book is applicable for use in introductory courses in women's studies and women and gender studies, and in upper-level courses in the field of women studies, gender studies, global gender studies, feminist economics, feminist critic, and political science, sociology, social work, and social studies that emphasize gender and development issues.

Gender within Global Development contains provocative issues that represent both sides—the developed and the developing world. It presents a comprehensive scholarly approach to questions concerning women in globally developing world.

Barbara Wejnert

Introduction

Popular books and textbooks dedicated to the analytical and theoretical understanding of the phenomena of **gender inequality** concentrate their investigations on the theorem of **gender** as a sole social entity. The studies include the analyses of the phenomenology of gender, the meaning and classification of gender, and perspectives and approaches to studies on gender. These types of studies can be classified as conceptual. At the same time, studies considered as applied concentrate on the application of the theoretical terms in research. Such studies explore, for instance, the relationship between gender and the surrounding social environment of the contemporary world, the impact of gender status on social positions of women and men within the global social setting, opportunities attainable by individuals, and the development of policies aimed at gender equality.

This book represents both categories of studies. It starts with a conceptual investigation of the meaning of gender, an analysis of different interpretations and explanations of gender, and inquiries on gender disparities. This conceptual discourse is followed by reflections on the opportunities for women's advancement that exist in the contemporary world. In this section, the importance of women's empowerment and the possibilities of its achievement are discussed using examples from the cross-cultural perspective. The final section of the book is devoted to comparative analyses of the opportunities open to men and women in developed Western countries versus developing countries of the global south.

The central argument of the book posits that gender gap is steady *increasing* across the world, despite current economic advancement, political freedom, spread of democratic ideology, the abundant flow of information, and increasing submersion of world's cultures. This phenomenon is counterintuitive to the expected and supposedly predetermined decline of gender disparity stimulated by global development. As frequently stated throughout the book, gender discriminatory stereotypes, patriarchal norms, and notions of dominant, hegemonic masculinity and emphasized femininity (Connell 1987) contribute to favoritism of one gender over the other, and provide a rationale for unequal treatment and biased practices against women. Visible examples of worldwide gender inequalities are divergent bargaining power, unequal access to control of societal resources, and imbalanced impact on development of major social structures and decision making. Global economic growth, planned as panacea for gender imbalance, has not reduced gender inequality across and within countries. On the contrary, it has increased the gender gap within countries and across the developed and developing world.

The central investigation of this book is preceded by an historical overview of the development of the concept of gender and its early interpretations. Reflections on theoretical approaches, their practical applications, and contemporary, global understanding of the theorem of global gender from cross-cultural perspective are guided by dialectic analyses.

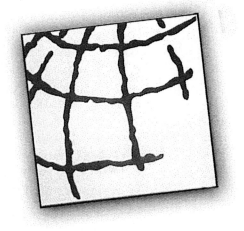

Biological and Socio-Cultural Perspectives on Gender

$\mathcal{I}$n what sense are men and women different, and in what sense are they similar? How can we define and measure differences between men and women? Are there any consequences of these differences for men and women? Is our everyday behavior, tastes, and desires; experiences in intimate relationships; health and well-being; career choices; and political beliefs linked directly or indirectly to gender? If men and women are physically and psychologically different in many aspects, can they be equal? Are women more equal to men in some type of societies than in others? What is the meaning of gender equality and gender gap?

Before we answer these questions and discuss how categories of sex and gender are defined, we must delineate the differences and similarities between men and women.

Sex versus Gender

Differences between men and women can be divided into biological, physiological, sexual, psychological, cultural, behavioral, and social (e.g., referring to a person's social position or social status). These various types of differences can be grouped into two main categories: **sex** and **gender.** These categories are often misunderstood; they are misinterpreted or viewed as having the same meaning. How can we differentiate and define what is sex and what is gender?

The World Health Organization defines *sex* as "the biological characteristics that define humans as female or male. While these sets of biological characteristics are not mutually exclusive, as there are individuals who possess both, they tend to differentiate humans as males and females" (World Health Organization 2002). Consequently, the category of sex interprets differences between men and women from a biological point of view. It depicts inborn differences, such as hormonal characteristics, body structure, reproductive organs, and genital characteristics. In popular terms, sex describes the meaning of being "a male" or "a female" and is used to refer to a person's biological maleness and femaleness (Newman 1997,141).

Gender, on the other hand, "refers to the economic, social and cultural attributes and opportunities associated with being male or female at a particular point in time" (World Health Organization 2001). Gender, therefore, depicts social and cultural differences between men and women that are defined and created by society and refer to societal roles constructed for women and man by and within society's culture. Consequently, gender is socially constructed and includes roles, behaviors, activities, and attributes that are considered appropriate for men and women. The power of gender lies not only in the cultural distinction of women and men and their social roles, but also in their designated ideological, political, and economic identity and their opportunities for social and economic advancement. Hence, gender can be regarded as the **master status** of each individual, overpowering any other roles that a person is expected to fulfill during their life course and guiding personal development (see Figure 1).

Master status, a term used to denote social position, identifies the primary characteristics of a person. It directs perception on what constitutes the typical male and female behavior (aggression versus nurturing) or traits (strong versus delicate), and is objictified to symbols colors

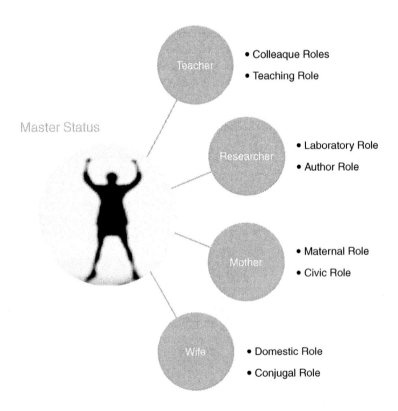

Figure 1. Illustration of the "master status" of a female faculty member

Gender status of a person defines and influences social roles that an individual plays in a society. It overpowers and supersedes any other descriptions that pertain to a personal identity of a man or a woman.

Sources: Figure designed by the author based on literal material from Maccioni (2005) and Marshall (1998)

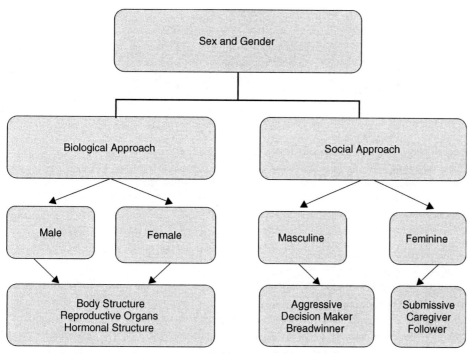

Figure 2. Conceptual model of the differences between sex and gender

Source: Figure designed by the author is based on the literal material on theoretical understanding of gender and sex (e.g., Bleier 1984; Connell 1987; Wilson 1975, 2000)

(pink versus blue) and material items (cars versus dolls). In popular terms, gender defines and compares what constitutes the meaning of being **feminine** or **masculine** (see Figure 2).

The cultural and social division of people on masculine and feminine has long-lasting consequences for women and men. Among the consequences are social inequalities expressed by economic and political opportunities, the perception of personal value, trajectory of life chances, bargaining power, access to and control of societal resources, and the security of well-being. Gender as the main status of each person overwhelmingly contributes to personal development and life chances. Although there may be differences across time and cultures as to how a particular society expects each gender to act and look, every society have some way of determining who is male or female, and teaches and reinforces the respectful form of feminine and masculine behavior (Newman 1997, 142–151).

On the global scale, gender is universal and cross-cultural. It is frequently argued that forms of masculinity and femininity are simplified to a single structural fact of a global "hegemonic masculinity." This structural fact provides the foundation for relationships among men and women. Accordingly, the dominant social group is masculine males, who have the broadest access to social, political, and economic resources. Males who behaviorally do not match the socially desired masculine type become subordinates, subjugated to masculine men, similar to all females who are globally subordinated to men. There is no femininity that is hegemonic; rather, the femininity is constructed to accommodate interests and desires of men, comprising the so called "emphasized femininity" (Connell 1987).

Figure 3. Promises of market economic system according to people needs

Source: This figure is an adaptation of segments of a cartoon published in "Moscow's Evening News" in early 1990s. The collage is designed by the author as a response to observed differences in economic experiences of men and women at the time of economic transition to a market economy in Russia.

Regardless of the many rights acquired by women since the beginning of the twentieth century, the gender gap persists across the contemporary world in terms of access to available resources, rights of men versus women, life chances and life choices, opportunities for advancement, and social perception of worthiness. Neither the gained women's rights to vote in the early twentieth century nor the recently increasing worldwide economic growth were able to eliminate or limit gender gap. Today, similarly to the past, women have limited access to societal and family resources, have limited rights within families, rarely are elected as national decision makers, earn much less income and own much less property than men, and have their decisions in a country or community viewed as less important than men's decisions. Across the world, gender inequality persists with patriarchal norms and stereotypes, contributing to a worldwide designation of social opportunities in favor of men. Societal attitudes toward gender are best captured by a created collage from cartoon characters of male and female promised to have their dreams fulfilled at a time of economic change, stimulated by a transition from a socialist economy to a market economy in Russia. As Figure 3 shows, men were promised to be proud owners of cars (rarely privately owned during communism), whereas women were promised to become involved mothers (as they were involved during communism). The post-communist transition led to a widening of gender gap and was particularly harmful to women.

Two or Three and More Gender

The gender characteristics that are associated with two biological sex categories, male and female, are assumed to be universal, comprehensive (i.e., there is no third sex), and mutually exclusive (i.e., a person cannot be both or be neither). Across cultures and time, societies may differ on behavioral characteristics designated to each gender; however, every society has a way of determining who is male and who is female—who is "either one or the other, 0 or 100 percent . . . we do not usually qualify it . . . If we should have to qualify it, then we seek further information until the qualification is no longer necessary" (Kessler & McKenna 1978, 2).

When individual sexual differentiation is not clear or is ambiguous because a person has the external genitals of one sex but the chromosomal pattern of another, or has partially one sexual category and partially another (like in cases of hermaphroditism), the medical community supports the cultural division of two sexes. "Hermaphroditism is usually defined by biologists as a combination of the two existing categories (of male and female) and not as a third, fourth, or fifth category unto itself. Furthermore, upon the diagnosis of Hermaphroditism, a decision is always made to define the individual as either male or female. In societies with advanced medical technology, surgical and chemical means may be used to established consistency between anatomy and the social label" (Newman 1997, 142). The medical interventions are not necessary from the point of view of an individual's health. They are performed only because social structure is organized according to two sexes.

Throughout history, only a few cross-cultural examples were found that illustrate patterns of more than two sex categories. In traditional Navajo culture, *Nadle* were individuals who were born with ambiguous sexual characteristics or who choose to perform the tasks of men and women. In a cultural tribe in Papua New Guinea, women and men lost feminine and masculine identities across their life cycle. Hence, older women were treated like masculine partners and were allowed to participate in tribal decision making, whereas older men with age lost their masculinity and acquired feminine status similar to young women. Indian culture permitted men born as men to undergo surgical removal of genitals to become Hijras, which is a man who behaves, dresses, and acts as a woman. Hijras had significant social status, power, and influence in society (Newman 1997).

Interestingly, in all of the above cultures, the new sex categories refer to sexual distinctiveness of male or female conforming to the inclusiveness and completeness of dual sexual division.

Transsexuals

In contemporary societies, an attempt to form a new sex category is represented by transsexuals—men and women who have the normal biological characteristics of one sex but gender identify with the other. Due to the inflexible gender patterns, altering gender is very complicated. For most individuals viewing themselves as transsexuals, it is easier to alter their sex with corrective surgery to make it match their psychological gender than to alter their gender to comply with sex characteristics.

In the United States and many Western societies, gender dichotomy is a way in which everyday life and larger social institutions are organized. Social institutions and ideological, religious doctrine reinforce the dual and differential gender status quo by awarding special rights and privileges to men over women. As a part of the differential treatment, women are banned from some positions of high prestige or power, such as ordination to priesthood, high clergy positions in Judo-Christian traditions (Chaves 1996), certain combat duties that create a path to a fast promotion, and some high profile professional sports (e.g., football).

Why, then, does gender gap still persist in modern societies?

Biological and Evolutionary Perspectives on Gender

The deterministic argument used against equality between male and female is rooted in biological differences between men and women, which are defined by sex. Until the twentieth century, scholars and philosophers alike were convinced that anatomic and hormonal differences between men and women determined gender roles and personality attributes.

Consequently, throughout history, a woman's physical body had been subject to scrutiny and evaluation. For example, St. Thomas Aquinas asserted that part of a woman's inferiority lies in her physical being. Aristotle's belief that women are "deformed men" doubtlessly influenced Aquinas' view of female inferiority. Women were seen as weak, brainless, and irrational imperfections of man. To prove the inferiority of women, scholars published statements in that favor. In 1879, Gustav LeBon wrote, "There is large number of women whose brain is closer in size to that of gorillas than to the most developed male brain. This inferiority is so obvious that no one can contest it for a moment. All psychologists who have studied the intelligence of women . . . recognize today that they represent the most inferior forms of human evolution and that they are closer to children and savages than to an adult, civilized man . . . . Without doubt there exist some distinguished women, very superior to the average man, but they are as exceptional as the birth of any monstrosity, as, for example, of a gorilla with two heads; consequently, we may neglect them entirely." (Gould 1980, 10–45). In 1971, T. Lang wrote, "It must be stated that conceptual thought is exclusive to the masculine intellect. Her skull is also smaller than men's, and so, of course, is her brain" (Wade and Tavris 1996, 336).

The historical notion of valueless womanhood was reborn in the United States in the 1970s, formulated by Edward Wilson's (1975) sociobiological approach to an understanding of human behavior. Wilson's approach upheld the genetic basis for all human behaviors. He emphasized that the female infant supposedly had greater dependence on parents, males were more aggressive and being right brain dominated, had superior visual-spatial skills in comparison to superior verbal abilities of left-brain dominated females.

In addition to biological determinism, an evolutionary approach was used as proof of female inferiority. Evolutionary explanations fell into four main categories:

1. *Sexual dimorphism, or male strength hypotheses,* explained that males are larger and stronger, have larger hearts and lungs, and possess less body fat. The greater strength of man was perceived as the superior evolutionary adaptation of males to the role of protection and providing associated with hunting. The physical strength supposedly made men superior over women.

2. *Male domination and bonding hypotheses* explained that males have a greater ability for social bonding than women do. This ability is genetically programmed and associated with working in decision-making groups, further augmenting men's power and prestige. Women, on the other hand, unable to bond together, are not suited for cooperative or political endeavors and are dominated by men who are the decision makers.

3. *Male aggression hypotheses* argued that males, by having high levels of testosterone (a male hormone), are more aggressive and thus dominate women (Bernstein et al. 1974, Mazur 1985, Rose 1978). More recently, this belief was restated and augmented by

an argument that a high level of testosterone is responsible for aggressiveness and dominance of men, which deters male occupational achievement (Dabbs 1992).

4. Lastly, *women childbearing hypotheses* stated that women desire to fulfill reproductive roles due to their inherent maternal instinct, hormonal characteristics, and natural attachment to children and family. Maternity requires the absence of women in nondomestic circles; hence, women depend on men for protection and provision and, in turn, submit to male needs to secure the survival of their offspring.

Only within the past few decades, biological and evolutionary perspectives have been scientifically disproved. Wilson's approach was contested by contemporary psychologists who suggested that male and female infants are undistinguishable by their degree of dependency on parents, and visual and verbal abilities. Therefore, any depicted behavioral differences are developed later in human life and, hence, must be a product of social influence (Bleier 1984, Fausto-Sterling 1985, Renzetti & Curran 1989).

Researchers also proved that there is very little difference in intellectual capabilities, abilities, or strength between men and women. The larger brain size of men, which had been used to cite as evidence of men's supposedly greater intelligence, was proved to be related to the average bigger body size of men than women. As was indicated, drawing inferences from biological differences about differences in behavior between sexes is not so easy, and thus they may be misleading (Deaux and Major 1990; Getz 2004, Reiter 1975).

Over time, evolutionary deterministic myths were also dispelled. The evolutionary theories of male strength failed under the critique of Leibowitz, who argued against the definition of strength exclusively as physical strength. Leibowitz stated that when one considers the dual approach to defining strength as physical and mental ability, women, who manage stress better than men and who, unlike men, being under stress withhold from despair, are equal if not stronger than men (Leibowitz 1989, 95–101).

Ehrenberg's critique denounced that the superior social position of men is a function of the uniqueness of male social bonding. Analyzing the sexual division of labor among early humans, Ehrenberg showed that early humans used bonding as a strategy for hunting (a male-dominated activity), as well as for gathering and child rearing, which were predominantly female activities. However, across time only men's activities were considered as entitled to the superior position. Moreover, reevaluation of the importance of women bonding during food gathering lead Ehrenberg to believe that hunting evolved from food gathering. Women's bonding, therefore, plausibly provided a model for male activity during the early division of labor (Ehrenberg 1989).

The hypothesis of a greater aggression of men was discussed by Lee (1979) in a study on differences in aggression level between and within sexes. The study disproved the deterministic view of male aggression resulting from a higher level of testosterone. The author argued that, in a great part, the difference lies in the cultural approval of a higher level of aggression for men than women, the difference in access to weapons, the cultural-approved expression of male hostility, and the role of status in evolution of social control. The cross-cultural data indicated that societies greatly vary in the approved level of aggression expressed by men and women; therefore, the high level of aggression of men must not only result from biology, but also from the culture of a particular society (Burbank and Robarchek, 1994). Clinical studies on infants also showed that the level of aggression measured by the infants' activity level is the same for baby boys and girls (Bleier 1984, Fausto-Sterling 1985, Renzetti & Curran 1989). Developing this notion further, Fausto-Sterling (1985) documented that studies on aggression and hormonal structure did not use female subjects and, hence, inference about differences between male and female aggression was unsound.

The final evolutionary explanation of maternal instinct possessed solely by women was questioned by researchers studying poor mothers who made selective choices to care only for the strong and healthy babies while neglecting or killing offspring who were weaker (Scheper-Hughes 1987); mothers who abandoned children who were sick (Boswell 1988); and mothers who sang lullabies, wishing death on sick babies (Ransel 1988). At the same time, patterns of strong attachments of mothers and fathers to infants were depicted in non-Western societies, disproving the hypothesis of male inability to be nurturing and natural caregiving (Hewlett and Lamb 2005).

To summarize the critique of biological and evolutionary explanations of existing gender gap, I incorporated data on the level of gender inequality demonstrated across societal development from gathering to post-industrial societies. As Figure 4 demonstrates, the level of inequality between genders varies across time, indicating that biological and

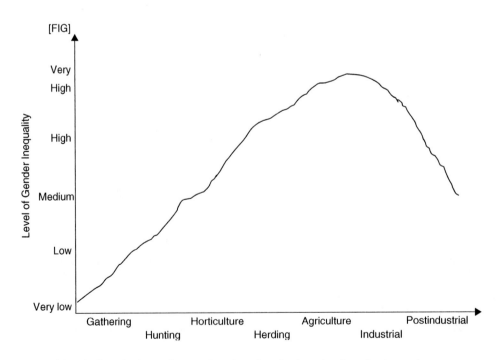

Figure 4. Level of gender inequality as a function of societal mode of production and sustenance
Source: Adopted from Chafetz (1984) and Huber (1986).

evolutionary differences between men and women have no uniform or universal impact on social roles. It is plausible to conclude that biological differences are unquestionable, but they depend on culture and societal structure as well as on biological characteristics.

Socio-Cultural Perspectives on Gender

The groundbreaking perspective in the biological interpretation of gender influenced Margaret Mead's studies on varied construction of gender among three neighboring tribes: the Arapesh, the Mundugumor, and the Tchambuli. In the Arapesh tribe, men and women were trained to cooperate and be unaggressive, caring, and responsive to the needs and demands of others (typical female behavior). In marked contrast were the attitudes of the Mundugumor, who were developed to be ruthless, aggressive, selfish, and unaffectionate. Among the Tchambuli tribes, Mead found a genuine reversal of sex roles, with women being the dominant, impersonal, and managing partner, and men being irresponsible and emotionally dependent. Mead found that in each culture, both men and women possessed characteristics that differed from one culture to another, and were almost entirely determined and constructed by differences in social and cultural conditions experienced by members of each tribe during childhood. Unlike her contemporaries, Mead argued that differences in behaviors were formed by culture, not by biological characteristics. This finding contradicted the notion of biological causes of personality traits used to define masculinity and femininity.

Mead's investigation was supported by Sapolsky's (1997) argument that testosterone level cannot account for aggressive behavior of men in contemporary societies because, if it did, the aggressive behavior of the Mungandor women would be impossible. Although Mead's studies were later broadly criticized, especially in terms of methodological accuracy and validity, she pioneered an array of research on the impact of society and culture on the perception of masculinity and femininity. In contrast to biologically oriented research attesting that biology and sex determine how the social role of men and women are designed, approved, and perceived, a new set of studies focused on the impact of local culture, customs, and values on the role and opportunities of each gender in a society.

For example, Messerschmidt (2006) stressed the significant differences among men and how men utilize different types of crime to construct distinct forms of masculinity. He explained that various forms of crime can serve as a suitable resource for dominating masculinity with the specific social context of the street, the workplace, and the family. Considering the environment of a street, Messerschmidt referred to a "deviant street network" as a suitable resource for masculine domination. The deviant street networks are groups of men and women assembled to conduct illegal, profit-making ventures such as prostitution, check and credit-card fraud, drug trafficking, burglary, and robbery. These networks are characterized by unequal gender relations. In most cases, women who equally participated in deviant activities turn their earnings over to the men in exchange for affection, an allowance, the status of their company, or safety and protection.

Furthermore, according to Messerschmidt (2006), masculinity and maleness is also used to reinforce man's power in the workplace.

Messerschmidt described that the macho sexual prowess, mediated through bravado and sexist joking, is constructed and encouraged on the shop floor. Failure to participate in this specific interaction raises serious questions about one's masculinity. For this reason, specific notions of heterosexuality are reproduced through the construction of shop-floor masculinity and sexual harassment, and center on men's insistence on exercising power over women. The workplace behavior of men is a reminder about "female fragility" that men use to discourage women from attempting to compete with them in the work domain.

Hegemonic masculinity is also reinforced in family relations and frequently takes a form of family violence. Violence in the household, according to Messerschmidt (2006), derives from the domestic authority of men, and is intimately linked to the traditional patriarchal expectation that man is the ruler at home and possesses the right to dominate the relationship. Men who beat their wives do not perceive violence as a crime, but rather they see it as a disciplinary act that would help the wife to be obedient and to ensure that male privileges are not unjustly denied.

Following these arguments, Connell (1987) believed that men have many reasons for complicity with the ideal cultural image of hegemonic masculinity and patriarchal gender stereotypes. Hegemonic masculinity is vital to male social status, promotion at work, wage structure, design of housing, taxation policy, family happiness, and self-worth. Hence, culturally constructed hegemonic masculinity is a powerful tool that molds behavior of men in every society. Conformation to the ideal model is strongly reinforced by agents of socialization including peer groups, family, school, workplace, and media. It is expressed in automobile advertisements, male cosmetics, sport and fitness equipment, liquors industry, and other "male" type of goods (Forrest 1989). The need to follow masculine cultural expectations is so strong that it often results in men's poor health. For instance, men learn to prove manhood through recklessness, involvement in contact sports, working in risky blue-collar occupations, and selecting endangering combat duties—all of which result in men having high injury rates. Similarly, traditional masculine behaviors associated with drinking, using drugs, and being sexually promiscuous elevate men's risks for early mortality (Sabo 2004).

Contrasting masculinity is subordinated femininity, which requires women to comply with their socially designated submissive roles and secondary social positions. Across various cultures, femininity is constructed in the context of the overall subordination of women to men, and is organized around sexual receptivity in relation to younger women and motherhood in relation to older women. Using the model of subordination, political institutions privilege men and exclude women from high posts and decision-making bodies. Economic institutions enforce women exploitation and discrimination, reinforcing an earning gap, creating unpaid women's work, and undervaluing domestic duties and caregiving. Gender discrimination of women is perpetuated not only in practice but also in everyday gendered language (e.g., high occupations only have masculine titles [lawyer, doctor, engineer, scientist]).

A study of men doing women's "pink" jobs (e.g., teachers, secretaries) demonstrated that rather than being surpassed by the larger number of women around them, these men experienced the "glass escalator effect," rising in disproportionate numbers to administrative jobs at the top of professions. As was hypothesized, a complex interplay between gendered expectations embedded in organizations (hegemonic masculinities) and the socially determined ideas workers bring to their jobs contribute to men's advantage in pink occupations (Williams 1989). It could be concluded that economic and political institutions act better toward non-conformist men categorized as the subordinated masculinities than toward women who are the subordinated femininity.

References

Bernstein, Irwin, Robert Rose, and Thomas Gordon. 1974. Behavior and environmental events influencing primate testosterone levels. *Journal of Human Evolution* 3: 517–525.

Bleier, Rith. 1984. *Science and gender: A critique of biology and its theories on women.* New York: Pergamon Press.

Boswell, J. 1988. *The kindness of strangers. The abandonment of children in Western Europe from late Antiquity to the Renaissance.* New York, NY: Pantheon Books.

Burbunk, V.K. and C.A. Robarchek. 1994. *Fighting Women: Anger and Aggression in Aboriginal Australia.* Berkeley, CA: University of California Press.

Chaves, Mark. 1996. Ordaining women: The diffusion of an organizational innovation. *American Journal of Sociology* 101: 840–873.

Connell, Robert, W. 1987. Hegemonic masculinity and emphasized femininity. In R. Connell, *Gender and power: Society, the person and sexual politics.* Stanford, CA: Stanford University Press.

Dabbs, James. 1992. Testosterone and occupational achievement. *Social Forces* 7(3): 813–824.

Deaux, Kay and Brenda Major. 1990. A social-psychological model of gender. In Deborah L. Rhode (ed.), *Theoretical perspectives on sexual difference.* New Haven: Yale University Press.

Ehrenberg, Margaret. 1989. *Women in prehistory.* Norman, OK: University of Oklahoma Press.

Fausto-Sterling, A. 1985. *Myths of gender.* New York: Basic Books.

Forrest, Thomas, R 1989. Such a handsome face: advertising male cosmetics. In Richardson, L. & Taylor, V.(eds.), *A feminist frontiers II: Rethinking sex, gender, and society.* New York: Random House.

Getz, Gene, and Elaine Getz. 2004. *The measure of a woman.* Ventura, CA: Regal Books.

Gould, Stephen Jay. 1980. The Panda's thumb. More reflections in natural history. W. W. Norton & Company.

Hewlett, Barry and Michael Lamb (eds.). 2005. *Hunter-gatherer childhoods: evolutionary, developmental, and cultural Perspectives.* Transaction Publishers

Kessler, Suzanne and Wendy McKenna. 1978. *Gender. An ethnomethodological approach.* Chicago, IL: Chicago University Press.

Lee, Richard. 1979. *The kung san: Men, women and work in a foraging society.* Cambridge, MA: Cambridge University Press.

Leibowitz, Lila. 1989. "Universals" and Male Dominance Among Primates: A Critical Examination. In Laurel Richardson and Verta Taylor (eds.), *Feminist Frontiers II.*

Macionis, John J. 2005. *Sociology.* Upper Saddle River, NJ: Pearson Education. (reference in Sources to Figure 1)

Marshall, Gordon (ed). 1998. *A dictionary of sociology.* New York: Oxford University Press.

Mazur, Allan. 1985. A biosocial model of status in face-to-face primate groups. *Social Forces* 64: 377–402.

Mead, Margaret. 1935, reprinted in 2001. *Sex and temperament in three primitive societies.* New York: Perennial.

Messerschmidt, James. 2006. Varieties of "real men." In Michael Kimmel and Michael Messner (eds.), *Men's lives.* London: Pearson Books.

Newman, David. 1997. *Sociology: Exploring the architecture of everyday life.* Thousand Oaks, CA: Pine Forge Press.

Ransel, David. 1988. *Mothers of Misery. Child Abandoment in Russia.* Princeton: Princeton University Press.

Reiter, Rayna. 1975. *Toward an anthropology of women.* New York: Monthly Review Press.

Renzetti, C.M., and D.J. Curran. 1989. *Women, men and society: The sociology of gender.* Needham Heights, MA: Allyn and Bacon.

Rose, Robert. 1978. Neuroendocrine correlates on sexual and aggressive behavior in humans. In Morris Lipton, Alberto Dimascio, and Keith Killam (eds.), *Psychopharmacology: A generation of progress.* New York: Raven Press.

Sabo, Don. 2004. Masculinities and men's health: Moving toward post-superman era prevention. In M. Kimmel and M. Messner (eds.), *Men's lives.* Boston: Allyn & Bacon.

Sapolsky, Robert. 1997. *The trouble with testosterone: And other essays on the biology of the human predicament.* New York: Scribner.

Scheper-Hughes, Nancy. 1987. The Cultural Politics of Child Survival. In Nancy Scheper-Hughes (ed.) *Child Survival.* Netherlands: Kluwer.

Wade, Carole, and Carol Tavris. 1996. Psychology. 4th ed. HarperCollins, New York, NY 336.

Williams, Christine L. 1989. *Gender differences at work.* Berkeley, CA: University of California Press.

Wilson, Edward, Osborne. 1975, reprinted in 2000. *Sociobiology: The new synthesis.* Cambridge, MA: Harvard University Press.

World Health Organization. 2001. Transforming health systems: Gender and rights in reproductive health. Retrieved on July 21, 2008, at http://www.who.int/reproductivehealth/gender/glossary.html.

World Health Organization. 2002. Gender and reproductive rights: Working definitions. Retrieved on July 21, 2008, at http://www.who.int/reproductivehealth/gender/sexual_health.html#1.

Name_____

Test Your Knowledge: Chapter 1

Short Answer Questions

1. The typical female role of a mother homemaker is to care for her children and husband, act obediently, and give her talents and devotion to the family. The typical male role as breadwinner is to be the decision maker for the family and authority figure to the spouse and children. Are these statements examples of the differences between sexes or the differences between gender? Explain your answer.

2. Do categories of feminine and masculine apply to gender or the sex? Explain your answer and provide examples illustrating each category.

3. Describe Margaret Mead's concept of gender roles when interpreting Sapolsky's and Messerchmidt theories of development of gender roles.

Multiple-Choice Questions

Instructions: Choose one answer to the following questions.

1. In the evolution from gathering to post-industrial societies, the degree of sex stratification:

   a. did not change.
   b. stately increased.
   c. declined only in post-industrial society.
   d. increased untill era of agricultural societies and declined since then.
   e. none of the above.

2. Margaret Mead's cultural studies in New Guinea show that gender roles are the result of:

   a. biological differences between men and women.
   b. the influence of society rather than biology.
   c. parental socialization.
   d. hormonal differences between tribes.

Macro and Micro-Social Perspectives on Gender

𝒯he macro-social perspective focuses on a trajectory, and the pattern and scope of societal development in order to understand gender-specific men and women behaviors. The main interest of scholars representing macro-social perspective is on the relationship between societal structures, such as social groups, organizations, and institutions (e.g., family, political, economic, religious, educational, and other institutions), and on how these relations change over time. Within the general perspective, three types of macro-social approaches that refer to gender can be denoted: **structuralism, functionalism,** and **conflict** (see Figure 5).

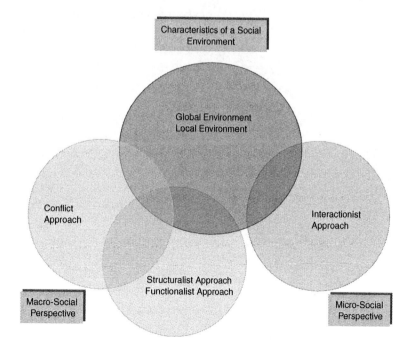

Figure 5. Impact of Social Environment on Macro and Micro Social Perspectives on Gender

Macro-Social Perspective on Gender: Structuralism

Scholars of the structuralism believe that societal structures profoundly shape human behaviors. Hence, they focus on how social groups, institutions, and societal culture, which define values and norms, influence gender roles expected to be performed by individuals. They also investigate men's and women's expectations and obligations in a particular society.

In the contemporary literature, several examples of structuralism as macro-social perspective on gender are depicted. A typical example of such studies is Messerschmidt's (2006) work delineating the meaning of "real men" in contemporary American society. The study states the nature of social institutions in which a man is embedded alters his behavior toward women. Accordingly, to follow expected social roles and to comply with prescribed masculine role, a man is encouraged to demonstrate his dominance, independence, assertiveness, strength, and aggressiveness. Such attitude frequently leads to his involvement in criminal activities. The study delineates this process when reflecting on "real men" behavior in three social environments:neighborhood community (described as the street network), workplace (depicted as a labor institution), and family (representing sexual institution).

Accordingly, the street network called "deviant street network" constitutes a group of men and women assembled to conduct illegal profit from prostitution, check and credit-card fraud, drug trafficking, burglary, or robbery. In this network, males and females are involved in criminal activity; however, men's illicit profit is kept by men, whereas women turn their illegal earnings over to men in exchange for affection, an allowance, the status of their company, or some measure of protection. Also, in exchange for the profit generated from women's earning, men acts as their agents. Any show of disloyalty by these women generates aggressiveness and violence of their agents.

To elucidate this situation, the study discusses a case of a female sex worker who was severely beaten up and wounded by her agent because she kept one night earnings for herself instead of giving them to the agent. The crime-prone, deviant street network fully approved the beatings and perceived it not as a criminal act, but as a lesson the sex worker needed to learn. Hence, in the street environment, men's absolute authority and control over women support the notion of masculinity (Mersserschmidt 2006).

In the environment of the workplace, masculinity, maleness, and men's power and control are also reinforced by men's aggressive behavior. The macho sexual prowess, mediated through bravado and sexist joking, is constructed and encouraged on the shop floor and failure to participate in this specific interaction raises serious questions about one's masculinity.

Women who enter the shop floor as co-workers are work competitors who threaten men's ego, assertiveness, and power. To discourage women from competition at work, men sexually harass women to remind them of their "female fragility." Most common types of sexual harassments are sexual slurs, pinches or grabs, and public displays of derogatory images of women (Messerschmidt 2006).

Messerschmidt noted that sexual harassment takes place also in the white, corporate world. Among one of the most typical situations is a male manager's sexual advancement toward a female secretary. In most cases, a manager would fire the secretary if she does not comply with the demanded sexual exploitation. Given the economic position of many women, termination, demotion, or not being hired is economically devastating (Messerschmidt 2006).

In the family, domestic violence is used as a behavior to support male masculinity. As Messerschmidt (2006) argues that, in a male opinion, wife beating is justified as a form of a discipline that helps the woman to be obedient and to make sure that male privileges are not unjustly denied. The wife beating and marital rape derives from the domestic authority of men, and is intimately linked to the traditional patriarchal expectation that men are heads and rulers of households and thus have a right to dominate marital relationship, including controlling women's sexuality.

Other studies examine the relationship between race/ethnicity and gender notions of masculinity and femininity in the United States. A study on African American, Hispanic, and Native-American men who are disproportionately poor, work in low-paying and hazardous occupations, and reside in high-crime, polluted environments are frequently exposed to toxic substances and to a hazardous life style. Nonetheless, they are the most common group that rarely has access to healthcare or medical services. As the study explains, the limitation or insufficiency of health services is in part a function of poverty, and in part stems from employment in industries without or with poor benefits. It is, however, also a result of a social stigma against ethnic and racial minorities. The stigma is expressed when healthcare providers are unwilling to offer sufficient medical care to minority men, such as African American men. In a particularly disadvantageous position are also gay men who face homophobia of healthcare workers. As another study explains, African American males have a great difficulty obtaining or keeping health insurance. Thus the African American males are considered the "endangered species" of a modern American society (Sabo 2004).

A typical example of a study that applies a macro-social perspective to understanding gender is Gilligan's (1997) study discussing the impact of socio-economic development and socio-economic system on gender roles. In his discourse on cultural behavioral patterns, values and practices in economically developed democracies that had evolved into "welfare states" since the end of the Second World War, Gilligan divided countries on wealthy but economically unequal and wealthy, economically equal. As he argued, in countries with large economic inequalities, the occurrence of gender violence (e.g., rape, domestic violence) is frequent contrasting states with a greater economic equality. In the author's opinion, violence is stimulated by shame and humiliation of male breadwinners who are unable to provide as high level of living for their families as the living standards provided by breadwinners who belong to wealthy social strata. In contrast, in well-developed countries with more equitable socioeconomic system, such as New Zealand, Australia and Japan, exist much smaller gap between the affluent and the less affluent social strata, and hence, the shame and humiliation felt among male breadwinners is minimal. As a result, in the United States, a country of economic contrasts, gender-related violent crimes occur two to twenty times as frequently as in any other similarly developed democracies.

The structuralist approach to understanding gender and gender-specific human behavior is frequently enhanced by a functionalist approach. According to this approach, gender roles and gender behaviors are shaped by societal structures and by functions of the structures. They are products of interdependency of structural forms and their societal functions and serve to preserves social equilibrium.

Macro-Social Perspective on Gender: Functionalism

Two types of gender roles organize society into well-functioning, cohesive organism:the hegemonic, dominant masculinity and the emphasized, subordinated femininity (Connell 1987). Behaviors are designed and expected from men and women following the general notions of a dominant masculinity and emphasized femininity.

Rooted in the tradition, cultural understanding of masculinity is the philosophy of "no pain, no gain" (Messerschmidt 2006). Subsequently, male athletes and men's sports are characterized by a tendency to glorify pain and injury, or to inflict injury on others to "win at all costs."

Football, for example, is as violent as hand-to-hand combat and can cause spine injury and brain damage. Nonetheless, football supports social order and approval of masculine aggressive behaviors. As it is explained in the United States, male athletic is a national ritual that upholds cultural values of competitiveness, toughness, and masculinity (Sabo 2004).

The "no pain no gain" viewpoint not only influences the quality of life, but also frequently jeopardizes the health of those who conform to its ethos. In many athletic activities, as well as combat duties and unsafe jobs, the injury is inevitable and sacrifices of health unavoidable. Men who are involved in these activities live shorter and are less healthy (Sabo 2004). Nonetheless, to secure the social equilibrium via masculinity and femininity notions, violent sport and hazardous working conditions are socially glorified (e.g., the hero football players or boxers, the hero firefighters or soldiers).

In America, like in many other countries, hegemonic masculinity requires a proof of manhood to gain social respect. To provide such proof, men engage in aggressiveness, antagonistic, hostile, and violent behavior, which is the underlying factors of masculine identity and for which they are honored. Consequently, men are honored for killing women, ethnic cleansing, spousal abuse, rape, sexual harassment, and other criminal or violent practices against women and accused of not being a true man when they are passive, gentle, and unwilling to be violent (Gilligan 2003). Many global practices of brutalizating women (Parrott and Cunning 2006) could be explained by this phenomenon.

On the other hand, economic and political organization of societies is also preserved by the cultural notion of women being submissive. This process is called by Connell "emphasized femininity" (Connell 1987). For instance, women experience greater difficulty than men in finding employment. Frequently, the only paid job is found in the informal labor market, which offers low-paying jobs with no or limited benefits, and hazardous or unsafe working conditions (e.g., sweat shops) (Tastsoglou and Hadjicostandi 2003). Similarly, any illegal work (such as work in the sex industry) could constitute the only open employment option (Mohanty 2003, McQuaig 1998, Perry A. & Mea 2002). In many countries, the informal labor market is vital to prosperous economic development because it reduces costs of production, lowers consumer prices, and, in turn, builds personal wealth and enlarges purchasing power of salary earnests. Thus, economic exclusion of women from access to available social resources, amplified by the exclusion from mainstream societal life, supports the omnipresent notion of subordinated femininity that helps to create social and economic equilibrium. For women, however, the main outcome of femininity is experienced sexism, prejudice, and discrimination on the labor market and in everyday life (Tastsoglou and Hadjicostandi 2003).

In many societies prevails the absurdity of a value system placing blame on women for potentially dishonoring men. In several cultures, such blaming leads to sentencing women to death if they are suspected to shame and disgrace honor of husbands or husbands' household (Parrott and Cunning 2006). In such situations, women's worthiness is judged as either honorable or shameful, depending on how well they perform or could perform roles of wives and mothers. Using these observations, Gilligan concluded that to prevent violence across the world, societies need to radically change gender roles to which men and women are subjected across the world (Gilligan 1997, 2001).

Macro-Social Perspective on Gender: Conflict

According to the founders of the macro-social perspective on gender (the conflict approach), the nature of society is inherently in a struggle between those who have access to power and resources and those who do not (Marx 1992, Engels 1884). Therefore, representatives of this approach argue that within and among social groups, organizations, and institutions (e.g., workplace, family, political organizations, schools and religious congregations) a conflict between men and women is perpetuated. This conflict is generated by a constant competition for resources, authority, supremacy, control, power, and social position.

A classic example of such studies is Karl Marx's belief that two separate spheres that are cultural determine and refer to gender roles, and bifurcate the lives of men and women in contemporary society are work and family. The gap in social positions of each gender stems from the type of work that is socially accepted, strongly desired, and, hence, universally performed by women. The work women concentrate on is at home. Private family life leads to the cult of woman as an unpaid domestic worker, caring for and servicing the needs of husbands and children, leading to women's marginalization. Tasks that women can perform outside of the domestic sphere are reserved for women only when men cannot perform them. Women thus constitute "a reserve army of labor" and oppressed social class (Marx 1992). The work of women in the form of subsistence work and in housework remains outside of the realm of paid labor and, hence, the debate on women's work is not related to the mode of production and accumulation as a whole.

At the same time, Frederick Engels analyzed families that emphasize a conflict between husbands and wives, especially in societies in which the main role of the wife is to perform housework. Competing for authority, status within family, dominance, control, and ownership of family's resources, housewives who are confine to home, engaged in housework, and taking care of children are subservient to husbands. Engels believed that women could be liberated only in an economic system in which they perform productive work and family duties if the system would support such development that women's housework constitutes only a minor part of their responsibilities. Such a system would need to support women's paid employment and, through appropriate policies, would need to facilitate a sharing of family care responsibilities with a developed network of family care institutions, such as nurseries and daycare facilities, afterschool program, nursing homes, system of public diners, public laundry facilities, etc. In a pre-capitalistic system, women's liberation was possible, because the community supported women's employment, offering help with family tasks. To end the conflict within family, enhance women's position, and end social inequality of women, family life needed to be removed from the private home and integrated with public life, allowing women to share some family care duties with family care institutions. Engels argued that in a capitalistic economy, which is most concerned with profit making, women's domestication and the limited employment of married women are unfeasible and, therefore, women's liberation and empowerment is impossible (Engels 1884).

Other studies emphasized women's exclusion from prestigious position, such as the exclusion of women from religious posts, among them ordination to priesthood, or high-level ministry (Chaves 1996) or from obtaining high paid jobs (Wagner, Ford and Ford 1986). Globally, despite the overall very demanding work load of women (Lewin et al. 2001), an earning gap persists between women and men (Kaufman 2002; Williams 1989). At present time, however, limited representation of women among political representatives and decision makers (Rueschmeyer 1998) does not project rapid changes of the situation.

The conflict perspective could be best summarized by a report of the United Nations Commission on the Status of Women (Morgan 1984). The report found that although women represent half of the global population and one-third of the labor force, they receive only one-tenth of the world's income and own less than one percent of world property. Women perform 60 to 80 percent of all agriculture work in the world and, in the developing countries, they produce more than 50 percent of the food supply (in African countries, more than 90 percent). Nonetheless, of 22 million people who die yearly from starvation, the majority are women and children under five years old.

Micro-Social Perspective on Gender

The most influential micro perspective is based on the interactionist theory that stems from socio-psychological concepts. Contrasting macro-social approaches, scholars representing the micro-social perspective believe that gender roles are not fixed and stable, but instead are unsettled, changeable, and irregular. Gender behavior is unstable and unpredictable because it is influenced by changing culture, whereas biological predispositions of men and women modify behaviors only to a minimal degree.

Because gender-related behavior is marked by flexibility, fluidity, and variability, men and women do not exhibit uniform behavior in various social situations. Instead, they choose to behave differently in varying social occasions, depending on a particular goal in a given inter-action, as the behavior is altered by the influences of another woman or man, by interactions with other people, and by the environment in which the interaction takes place. For example, a woman presenting her-self to a man with socially desirable characteristics would modify her behavior to approximate the man's expected views. In contrast, when a man posses traits that would presumably not motivate continuation of interactions, a woman would alter her behavior to be perceived as unde-sirable. Thus, there are no steady characteristics that are strictly female or male and are culturally or biologically imposed. People choose to self-present themselves with a certain kind of motivation. As humans, we have identities other than male and female, so we are more prone to incorporate all identities that we possess into one behavior and act for the sake of goals, including goals that are not recognized in conscious light (Deaux and Major 1990). Thus, there are no steady and typical female or male behaviors that are culturally or biologically imposed across societies. Contrarily, individuals select the most suitable behav-iors for them in a particular situation. In interactions with others, people choose to present themselves based on motivation to continue or end interaction. A broad set of characteristics that each person possesses, including being female or male, are incorporated into the behavioral act. The behavior is altered according to personal goals that an individual has in a particular interaction or social environment. As the scholars of this approach believe, this process also occurs in situations when goals are not consciously recognized.

A typical example of this theoretical approach is when people, in-teracting with others, undertake roles of performing actors rather than exposing real feelings or attitudes that they may have. The social roles of men and women change, reflecting the circumstances of the social situa-tion and meaning that a particular person attaches to received stimuli and symbols, such as a look of the interacting partner. In social interac-tions, men and women respond to those meanings, or symbols. A person acts in a particular way, depending on the social circumstances that the person is exposed to at a particular time, and actively selects behaviors that are the most suitable for that particular situation.

References

Chaves, Mark. 1996. Ordaining women: The diffusion of an organizational inno-vation. *American Journal of Sociology* 101: 840–873.

Connell, Robert. 1987. Hegemonic masculinity and emphasized femininity. In R. Connell, *Gender and power: Society, the person and sexual politics.* Stanford, CA: Stanford University Press.

Deaux, Kay and Brenda Major. 1990. A social-psychological model of gender. In Deborah L. Rhode (ed.), *Theoretical perspectives on sexual difference.* Yale University Press.

Engels, Frederick. 1884, reprinted in 1972. The origin of the family, private prop-erty and the state. *Selected works: MECW*, Volume 26. Hottigen-Zurich.

Gilligan, James. 1997. *Violence: Reflections on a national epidemic.* New York: Vintage Books.

_____. 2001. *Preventing violence.* New York: Thames and Hudson.

_____. 2003. Culture, gender, and violence: "We are not women". In M.S. Kimmel and A. Aronson (eds.). *The gendered society reader.* New York, NY: Oxford University Press.

Kaufman, R. 2002. Assessing alternative perspectives on race and sex employment segregation. *American Sociological Review* 67: 547–572.

Lewin, James, R. Weisell, S. Chevassus, C. Martinez, B. Burlingame, and A. Coward. 2001. The work burden of women. *Science* 294, October.

Marx, Karl. 1992. *Capital: A critique of political economy.* New York: Penguin Press.

McQuaig, Linda. 1998. As long as they can sell their blood. In Heiner (ed.), *Social problems and social solutions.* Boston, MA: Allyn & Bacon.

Messerschmidt, James. 2006. Varieties of "real men." In Michael Kimmel and Michael Messner (eds.), *Men's lives.* London: Pearson Books.

Mohanty, Chandra T. 2003. *Feminist without borders: Decolonizing theory, practicing solidarity.* Durham, NC: Duke University Press.

Morgan, R. 1984. *Sisterhood is global.* New York: Anchors Books.

Parrott, Andrea and Nina Cummings. 2006. *Forsaken females.* New York, NY: Rowman and Littlefield.

Perry A., and Mea Sai. 2002. How I brought two slaves to free them. *Time,* March 11.

Rueschmeyer, M. 1998. *Women in the politics of postcommunist Eastern Europe.* New York: Sharpe.

Sabo, Don. 2004. Masculinities and men's health: Moving toward post-superman era prevention. In M. Kimmel and M. Messner (eds.), *Men's lives.* Boston: Allyn & Bacon.

Tastsoglou, Evangelia and Joanna Hadjicostandi. 2003. Never outside the labor market, but always outsiders: Female migrant workers in Greece. *The Greek Review of Social Sciences* 110: 189–220.

Wagner, David, Rebecca Ford, and Thomas Ford. 1986. Can gender inequalities be reduced. *American Sociological Review* 51(1): 47–61.

Williams, Christine. 1989. *Gender differences at work.* Berkeley, CA: University of California Press.

Name_____

Test Your Knowledge: Chapter 2

Essay Questions

1. Describe the differences between the structuralist and interactionist theories in application to the gender perspective, and interpret the text below with an application of each theoretical understanding.

   At the start of the U.S. involvement in the WWII efforts, American men were drafted to the army, and vacant industrial positions needed new employees. Through broadly spread advertisement, women were encouraged and welcomed to take vacant jobs, and a new role model of a hero working women and working mother was advertised.

   After the war, returning soldiers returned to their former jobs, and women were dismissed from the work force. Women employment was unneeded and hence unwelcomed. A new image of women as homemaker and a procreator was advertised in the American media, frequently stressing how devastating women's employment is to children.

   In your interpretation, using one of the discussed theoretical perspectives on gender, focus on changing socio-economic and political conditions of the United States that were reflected in changing patterns of women's roles.

Multiple-Choice Question

Instructions: Choose one answer to the following questions.

"In the pre-industrial societies, which depended on hunting and gathering, men and women fulfilled different roles and took different tasks because to do so was useful and necessary for the whole society to survive."

What sociological perspective rests on the belief stated above?

a. functionalist
b. conflict
c. interactionist
d. none of the above

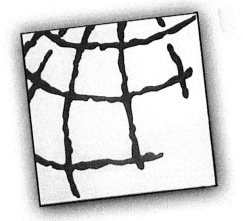

3

Feminist Theories of Gender

Definition of Feminism and Feminist Theory

Feminism is defined as the belief that women have equal political, social, sexual, intellectual, and economic rights as men do. Within this framework, theorists and activists discuss the concept of gender equality and advocate for women's earning power, education, political and civil rights, economic and social power, and domestic rights equal to men. It is a discourse that involves scholars representing various philosophical perspectives, including literature, philosophy, economics, psychoanalysis, sociology, anthropology, history, political science, aesthetics, and art.

The concept of feminism led to the formation of **feminist theory**, which aims to understand the nature of gender inequality and emphasizes gender politics and power relations between sexes. While generally providing a critique of social relations, the ultimate goal of feminist theory is to analyze and delineate gender politics, power relations, and sexuality in contemporary societies to form foundations for activism and developing the feminist movement. Within this framework, members of the feminist movement campaign for women's rights and interests, and for the improvement of women's well-being worldwide.

Historical Development of the Feminist Movement

Feminist movement struggles to defend and expand the rights of women. It was initiated in France during the French Revolution of 1789 in Paris, where women's club were formed. During the club's meetings, the first political program regarding women's rights that called for women rights to education, employment, and political representation in the state government was developed. The rights were declared in the first official document, the "Declaration of the Rights of Women," written by Maria Gouze under the pseudonym Olympe De Gouges. Unfortunately, reaction to this document indicated the attitude of male-dominated society toward women's rights. Maria Gouze's ideas on gender equality were considered subversive and dangerous, and she was put to death by the guillotine in 1793. The executioners charged her for forgetting the virtues belonging to her sex. Such strong reaction to the idea of gender equality was an indication of the struggle awaiting the women's rights movement.

Throughout the history, three consecutive waves of the feminist movement emerged, each representing a distinct set of goals and different type of women's groups. Initially, the movement represented the concerns of women of the middle and upper class from Western societies, but in the last wave grew, incorporating complex transnational and global problems.

First-Wave Feminism. In the first decade of the1900s, at the beginning of movement's development, feminist theorists and activists primarily concentrated on securing basic political and economic rights of women. The most visible rights were the right to own property and have property contracts equal to men, the political right to vote (right of women suffrage), and the right to oppose marriage when married women and their offspring were owned by husbands.

The first wave feminists consisted of mainly white, middle-class women who represented the interests of the middle class. Their agenda could be summarized as a struggle to achieve formal, legal equality for women, and to grant the right of citizenship. Through pressure on politicians and non-violent protests, suffrage activists, including prominent Susan B. Anthony, Elizabeth Cady Stanton, Lucy Stone, Olympia Brown, and Helena Pitts, overcame the opposition of conservative forces to broaden the scope of citizenship in Western Europe—notably France and England—and in the United States. During this wave, the feminist movement took primarily a **maternalistic approach** to women's identity, referring to and identifying with the image of women as the Virgin Mary and focusing on the moral qualities women possess (Freedman 2003). Only some feminists, like Margaret Sanger and Voltaire de Cleyre, actively campaigned for broader rights, including reproductive rights and economic rights. Not surprisingly, gains achieved within the first wave mainly pertained to white, middle- and upper-class women.

Second-Wave Feminism. The most important feature of the second wave of the feminist movement was the recognition that the power of women should be found in private and public life. This wave, which lasted from the 1960s to the 1990s, was a period of promoting equal rights and ending women's discrimination in public and domestic spheres. Eisenstein (1983) noticed that this change from the personal to the political appeared in two steps. First, women's subordination began to be seen as political and social—not as individual oppression but as a force that was operating in society at large to perpetuate the subordination of women as a class (Eisenstein 1983, 38). In the 1960s and 1970s, feminists began to address several of the critical issues women faced in a patriarchal society:tackling the issues of sexual harassment, wage inequality, sexual discrimination, women's healthcare issues, education, reproductive rights, domestic violence, and pornography. Conscious-raising groups became a means for feminists to share their experiences and feelings of oppression under male domination. As the number of groups grew, women began to see their shared experiences and realized they were not alone, which enabled them to bring the private sphere into the public realm through public campaigns and political activism in the second part of the second wave. Consequently, building on the developed agendas of the 1960s and 1970s, political activism led to the formation of a women's movement with elements of political organization. Political activity, in turn, became the substance of the women's movement (Eisenstein 1983, 38). Promoted rights and ideology criticized the profoundly ingrained, powerful notion that women find personal fulfillment only through childbearing, domestic duties, and homemaking, and that women's identity and the meaning of their life comes through the accomplishments of children and husbands. Feminist opposing such notions portrayed a woman's separate identity not related to family members (Friedan 1963).

In addition, the second wave of feminism promoted the cultural understanding of women's value as intertwined with political and economic structures and with culture of inequalities. Therefore, feminists encouraged women to understand their personal life as a politicized outcome of the sexist power struggle (Hanisch 2006). For example, the technological advancements of the post–WWII period, which eased domestic work and replaced part of women's domestic labor, lowered the perception of women's worth at home and diminished the societal value of women because opportunities for advancement in non-domestic spheres were limited.

Broad agenda of the second wave incorporated such divers issues as women's paid employment, regardless of being married or single women; breaking the glass ceiling in job promotions; securing access to political power for women; provision of day-care centers; access to planned parenthood, birth control, and abortion; breaking salience about rape, sexual violence, and domestic violence; making divorce available to women; making it acceptable for women to choose single life as an alternative to marriage; acceptance of relations with the same sex partner; and acceptance of women's childlessness.

Despite its much broader agenda, the second wave of feminism was criticized for its limited contributions to the advancement of women and to women empowerment. It was criticized for its limited scope of concerns for different social classes and ethnic and racial groups, while focusing on only white, middle-class women. Also criticized was its limited impact on governments' promotion of social equity and opening of opportunities for women's individual progress and development (Watkins 1984).

Thus, the second wave of feminism eventually split into two distinct branches, one focusing on the access and influence on societal institutions to introduce gender equality, and another skeptically withdrawing from societal culture and opposing inclusion of women in existing patriarchal institutions. In the latter approach, a separate women-only space was designed as an open, available space for women's activity. This branch eventually led to the appearance of differentiated identity politics and identity feminism.

Third-Wave Feminism. The third-wave feminist movement, which was born out of the first- and second-wave feminism, responded to the limitations of the second wave by opposing the pro-white, upper-, and middle-class Western view on women's identity and her position in social life. It challenged the essentialist approach to woman as characterized by identical sets of qualities.

At the same time, the movement's leaders encouraged women to perceive themselves as capable, assertive, and empowered to introduce changes. For example, in the 1980s Third World feminists began to research poverty from a gendered perspective commonly known as the "feminization of poverty." Diana M. Pearce introduced the phrase *feminization of poverty* in her 1978 research paper, which stated that women comprised more than 66 percent of the poor over 16 years of age at that time (McLanahan 1985). Although more women had entered the work market in the 20 years between 1950 and 1970, their economic status had deteriorated.

Pearce viewed the feminization of poverty as twofold. First, she believed that women's poverty differs from that of men. Secondly, she believed that the programs offered to help poor women escape poverty were developed for poor men, not poor women. Working at any job, even though it may be at minimum wage, is not sufficient to escape poverty (Pearce 1978). Searching for explanations of the feminization of poverty, Pressman (2003) states that women are more likely to be poor than men as a matter of established structural organization of societies.

Female poverty is unique because of women's responsibility for children and discrimination in the labor market, so that employment cannot be the only solution for women (Gordon 1994. Thus, poverty and inequality of women in comparison to men has increased poverty among children. In female-headed households with children, nearly two-thirds of all children were at the bottom of the family income distribution (Lichtner et al. 1997).

Importantly, not only were female head of households seen as having higher poverty rates, but also the length of time that they endured poverty most likely was long-term (NCCP 2007).

Therefore, during the third wave, the typical concerns of feminism addressed problems of women's political and civil rights (e.g., women's representation in governing bodies), extended by issues of reproductive rights, including the promotion of family planning and abortion rights; civil rights and laws to end violence against women, including sexual harassment policies and bringing to light the frequency of sexual and domestic violence against women; equal access of women to any field of education; and rights to perform any type of job and to "equal pay for equal work," affordable childcare, and affordable health care. These main issues stimulated the development of sets of specific concerns, including the ability for women to have high-paying jobs; getting women into position of economic power; changing family and work structure to limit daycare use; freeing leisure time for mothers; breaking salience about consensual sex and same-sex relations, making heterosexual marriage a better choice for women who want it, but opening possibility for non-heterosexual marriage; and increasing earning power to allow women to be mothers. The third wave of feminism was represented by a feminist movement that aimed at a practical implementation of philosophical and theoretical explanations that seem to complicate our understanding of the second wave of feminism. Representative of this wave not only embraced the second wave critique of beauty culture, sexual abuse, and power structures as the movement's agenda, but also focus on ways that desires and pleasures such as beauty and power can be used to enlighten and cheer up activist work (Heywood and Drake 1997) (see Table 1).

Representatives of this wave emphasized cross-cultural perspective rejecting the nation of universal womanhood. The only exception was for the omnipresence of patriarchy (control of man) across world's societies.

TABLE 1. REQUESTED RIGHTS FOR WOMEN AS OBJECTIVES OF EACH WAVE OF FEMINIST MOVEMENT

FIRST WAVE	SECOND WAVE	THIRD WAVE
Right to vote (suffrage)	Right to employment, regardless of marital status	Right to equal pay for equal job
Right to own property	Right to professional advancement (breaking the glass ceiling)	Right to hold economic power by women
Right to the same ownership contracts as men have	Right to hold position of political power	Right to flexible job time to limit day care use
	Right to loving sexual relationship with other women	Right to high salaries and highly professional job
	Right of mothers to work	Right to employment in any job in which men are employed
	Right to abortion and family planning	Right to have homosexual relationships (including transsexuals)
	Opening day-cares	Breaking salience about need for consensual sex
	Breaking salience about violence against women (eg., rape and sexual abuse)	Right to open access to all social opportunities
	Right to divorce, single parenthood, childlessness	

The patriarchal system promoted dominance of men over women in the same way as dominance of men over the environment was promoted. Accordingly, men's exploitation of women for their own profit was seen as similar to men's exploitation of the environment.

Such a perspective stemmed local, national, and transnational activism. Actions organized by feminist activists emphasized an end to sex trafficking, body surgery, pornography, woman sex slavery, as well as the abolishment of sweatshops, devaluation of woman work, and the absence of women's rights in domestic spheres. Over time, the broadening constituencies that the movement represented led to the split of the univocal feminism movement into branches according to particular sets of principles relevant to represented constituencies.

Thus, the third wave, stemming from global development, was not universal or unified. Rather, it constituted clusters of feminist trends and groups concerned with the theoretical understanding of womanhood and feminist philosophy. Among these trends was **postmodern**

feminism, which incorporated postmodern philosophy and poststructuralist theory. Its departure from feminism was marked by the argument that gender is constructed through language. Emphasizing language and its reference to women identity, representatives of this group (e.g., Judith Butler, Mary Joe Frug) argued against language distinction between biological sex and socially constructed gender, believing that it narrows the complexity of the meaning of "woman." Accordingly, it was argued that being a woman is defined not only by biological sex, but also by class, race, ethnicity, and sexuality, among other characteristics. Some of the representatives of this group, who followed the postmodern philosophy, argued that women are brought up in a world defined by men. In this world women are considered not normal and the 'Other' and while the norm is to be a male, femaleness is outside the norm (de Beauvoir 1972). Women activity takes place only within a society defined in such way.

Responding to the criticism of Western, middle-class bias, **multiracial feminism** focused on the life and experiences of women of color. Representative to this trend was Chicana feminism (e.g., represented by the work of Maxine Baca Zinn) and African American feminism (represented by Dr. Bonnie Thornton Dill).

Overall, the third wave of feminism focused on the development of feminist theory and politics that aimed to deconstruct the former categorical thinking in terms of woman (us) and man (them). The former approach followed stereotypical thinking in terms of gender roles and did not envision improvement of sexist society or condemning sexist stereotypes. To underline the new approaches, feminists of the third wave exaggerated sexist stereotypes by inventing new language and new forms of communication that parodied and humorously mimicked sexist stereotypes.

Classification of Feminist Theories According to Represented Constituencies

Feminist movement started with **Western feminism**. Established mainly by middle-class, white women from Western Europe and North America, this segment of feminism called for the end of gender discrimination at home, in the workplace, and in political and social arenas. It was concerned with a broad set of women's legal rights (rights of contract, property rights, voting rights). Over time, it added women's right to bodily integrity and autonomy, abortion rights, and reproductive rights (including access to contraception and quality prenatal care) to its concerns. Among other concerns were legal rights, such as protection from violence against women, domestic violence, sexual harassment, and rape; legal rights to social security related to women's well-being; and the right to maternity leave and equal earning capacity (i.e., "equal pay for equal work").

The main objective of Western feminism was to combat the various forms of gender discrimination experienced by women from Western societies. Publicized feminist theory proclaimed that gender oppression primarily results from dominant patriarchy, where in a social system men are regarded as the authority within the family and society and, therefore, power and possessions are rest and hold in men's hands. Although the movement manifested its agendas across the world and in principle, the set of demanded rights seemed to be inclusive of all races and ethnicities. In practice, however, it pertained to issues mainly concerning middle-class, white women.

As early as 1851, with the speech of black feminist, Sojourner Truth's, the existing feminist understanding of gender inequality was challenged by an alternative **Black feminism** approach. This branch of feminism argued that sexism, class oppression, and racism are intertwined and, hence, black women experience oppression differently and more intensely than white women. The perception of gender discrimination that includes all women should incorporate the end to class oppression, racism, and sexism. Subsequently, Western feminism born in Western culture was accused of ethnocentrism, in particular of entertaining the belief that cultures of white race and of white ethnic groups are the most important and superior to those of other groups. Nonetheless, the objectives of Western feminism provided the foundation for the expansion and incorporation of issues specific to women of other races and of non-Western societies.

Post-colonial feminism opened a period of opportunities to the development of feminism representing voices of women in the Third World. Post-colonial feminists, represented by Chandra Talpade Mohanty, constituted one of the groups of the third wave of feminism. These feminists argued that colonial experiences of women—especially race, ethic, and class oppression—marginalize women in post-colonial countries. Representatives of this theory challenged the assumption that patriarchy is the primary force influencing experiences of women. In post-colonial states, historical marginalization of women during colonial time added to the patriarchal effect in forming life circumstances of women in post-colonial countries.

Gender inequality stemming from post-colonial experiences provided the framework for the agenda of post-colonial feminism. This agenda included (1) opposition to the Western notion that gender oppression is the primary potency strength of a broadly spread patriarchy; (2) opposition to control and monitoring of the status of women and their well-being by Western organizations and former colonial power while using Western standards; and (3) opposition to the imposition of Western norms on former colonial dependencies, including women's roles and behaviors. Such opposition was particularly important when one considers that submission to traditional practices and women's roles, which often contradicted the Western model of womanhood, was a form of rebellion of women from the developing countries against colonial oppression. Another objective was on the struggle against gender oppression within cultural models of their own societies rather than through those imposed by the Western colonizers.

Classification of Feminist Theories According to Represented Objectives

The complexity of issues and demands requested by women representing various socio-economic strata, race, ethnic groups, and cultures initiated a variety of feminist theories that could be broadly divided according to the descriptive questions and explanatory answers of "What about women?" and of "Why is the women's situation as it is?" (Lengermann and Niebrugge-Brantley 1992).

Within the first set of theoretical suppositions are **theories of difference, of inequality,** and **of oppression.** The first type of theories suggests that women's life experiences are different than that of men. The differences result from biological differences between men and women, and from social roles required of women and men to perform for security, stability, and sustainability of societal existence. The theories of differences refer to differential placement of women, in comparison to men, within society and differential roles played within social, political and cultural institutions, such as, family, workplace, schools, religious institutions (e.g., places of worship, religious hierarchy), and governments (see Table 2). An explanation of the differences between men and women rely on the general understanding that the gender roles are determined by the biological differences that women and men are born with, such as prolonged dependence of females on their family of origin, women's strong ability to care and feel compassion, and greater verbal capabilities in left-brain dominated women, which contrast to the analytical abilities of right-brain dominated men.

The second set of theories explained that women not only differ from men, but also that women are treated *unequally* to men. This inequality is expressed as less privileged and unequal societal experiences of woman versus man. As liberal explanations argued, the inequality is caused by wrongly established social, legal, and political laws, regulations, and institutions. It was believed that reforms of the legal system and social policies would alleviate the inequality. To better accommodate gender equality, societal institutions and organizations need to undergo a transformation so women are able to fully explore and express their abilities. These reforms should be instituted within an existing structure of society jointly by women and men.

A more extreme position was taken by **Marxist feminists,** immersed with Marx and Engels teaching on class oppression. Extending the class

TABLE 2. CLASSIFICATION OF FEMINIST THEORIES ACCORDING TO OBJECTIVES

WHAT ABOUT THE SOCIETAL POSITION OF WOMEN? (THEORIES)	WHY IS WOMEN'S POSITION AS IT IS? (EXPLANATIONS)
Theories of difference (women are different than men)	Bio-social explanation, institutional explanation, social-psychological explanation
Theories of inequality (women are unequal to men)	Liberal, feminist explanation; Marxian explanation
Theories of oppression (women are oppressed by men)	Psychoanalytical explanation, radical feminist explanation, socialist feminist explanation, third-wave feminist explanations of oppression

Sources: Compiled and modified from Lengermann and Niebrugge-Brantley 1992.

oppression into the notion of women oppression, representatives of this perspective blamed the exploitative social system that uses one societal group for the benefit of others, discriminatory practices, and creation of unequal social structures. In this sense, focusing on the low valuation or non-valuation of women's work in public and private spheres, representatives of this approach looked at women as one social class in which gender relations are embedded in a more fundamental structure of class system. Women's quality of life and gender equality reflect primarily the class position, whereas is less influence by the fact of being women or men. It would be possible to imagine that men and women in the same social class of working poor, middle class or upper, wealthy class would hypothetically experience more similar life circumstances than women belonging to different classes. Similar to the working poor, who were used and oppressed by a powerful class of capitalists, women within the working class were being kept down by capitalists who were patriarchal rulers. In this sense, gender inequality was reduced to inequalities experienced by classes.

Stemming from the perspective of oppression was the last set of explanations that argued not only for women inequality but their abuse, subordination, and use by men. The complex oppression helps to mold women's personalities to be subordinate and obedient to male control, decreases sense of worth and value in own abilities, and alters women's achievement. Three distinct subcategories dominated this theoretical explanation: **psychoanalytic**, **radical feminist**, and **radical socialist approach**.

The psychoanalytic explanation of oppression reworks the patriarchal conclusion made by Freud, which can be summarized by the blunt statement that women are second class-citizens because gender is a base of psycho-sexual development of individuals. Gender inequality is developed in early childhood in relation to men's desires to be masculine. Boys copy masculine roles of fathers as dominating individuals, and girls copy mothers trying to be feminine and, as mothers, to be subordinated to males. Furthermore, following Freud's psychoanalytic theory, women's oppression is a result of men's deep desire to control women. This desire is generated by the male's Edip complex and fear of death, leading to control of women's procreative behaviors. Gender described by such principles alters the individual psycho-sexual development of women and men.

Like Marxist feminist approach, the radical socialist approach analyzes women's experience of subordination as relating to the capitalist patriarchy, which induces various forms of oppression of social groups and strata, including the oppression of women. In contrast to the Marxist approach, representatives of this theory believed that women's oppression should be separated from class oppression because eliminating class oppression will not ultimately eliminate women's oppression. The goals and objectives addressing women's oppression should not be merged with class oppression.

The third wave of feminism represented discourses on the positions of women in various countries. One of the examples was feminist movement in Poland (see box).

Feminist Struggles in Poland

by Joanna Regulska, Rutgers University

Polish women secured voting rights in 1918. This places Poland among the early wave of the European countries that responded positively to women's demand for political rights. The initial suffragist mobilizations began toward the end of the nineteenth century. As Polish state did not exist at that time, the struggle for women's political rights was not a priority. Women focused instead on securing rights of access to higher education and employment. The creation of the Flying University in Warsaw in 1905 is one example of how such demands were translated into action. The 1917 congress of women—which took place illegally and underground—was critical in the process of securing voting rights for women. The 200 women, representing all three partitions of Poland (Russia, Prussia, and Austria), came together to press for change. By electing five representatives, who in turn negotiated with General Piłsudski for voting rights "without sex differentiation," Polish women became visible political subjects. In 1921, the Polish Constitution reconfirmed women's voting rights (eFKA 2007).

These and other examples of women's activism contradict the often-heard argument that the women's movement is young and dispersed, or that there is no feminist mobilizations in Poland (Graff 2001). A long history of struggles in the early years of the twentieth century, engagement in defeating the communist regime or sustained mobilizations, albeit unsuccessful, during the 1990s to counter Church and the State attacks on women's reproductive rights all in fact indicate the actual strength of women and feminists in organizing and pressing for social change (Jacquette 2003; Lukić, Regulska, Zaviršek 2006; Penn 2005). One of the reasons why women's mobilizations often remain unacknowledged is the unequivocal connection between the history of the nation and that of the women's movement in Poland (Fuszara 2006). The nineteenth century struggles to secure political rights were certainly overshadowed by the lack of Polish statehood. More recently, in the 1980s when martial law was implemented and especially after 1989, arguments have been made that women have to wait until more critical socio-economic concerns that affect the entire nation will be resolved first.

The period of communism brought mixed results for women. Despite the rhetoric of equality, it did undoubtedly restrict women's autonomy. In practice, this meant for women massive participation in the production sphere, combined with pressures and responsibilities to fulfill reproductive and caring duties. The images of "women on tractors" (the heroine worker and the heroine mother) created a socialist gender regime that *de facto* was based on deeply rooted gender inequalities. For Polish women to be emancipated meant to produce, reproduce, and provide care. It meant to carry a double or triple burden. The project of emancipating women aimed as much to aid the expansion of the working class as to justify the imposition of set of controls and duties over women to fulfill the needs of the paternalistic state.

Despite many unquestionable gains such as women's educational achievements, their greater access to social benefits and their entry into the labor force, as well as inequalities were visible. The persistence of gender occupational segregation, wage gap, and income inequalities are just a few of the key factors indicating that socialist project, contrary to its proclamations of equality, ultimately was not interested in gender equality and that its policies aided the reproduction of inequalities. Yet, the total rejection of the socialist gender regime, without the recognition of its contributions to the improvement of women's position, would be unjustified. The paternalistic socialist state generated numerous policies that advanced women and provided them with wide-ranging services and benefits. The *en mass* opening of educational opportunities to women across all levels created a phenomenally high level of educational attainment among women. In the end, however, did it make a difference for women?

Scholars argue that while making gender difference an ideological tool of the communist propaganda, the previous regime led to the erosion of the sense of a bond between women as a group (Bator 1999). This resulted in women's unwillingness to articulate their interests in terms of the group interests; they rejected all kinds of group identity and perceived feminism as "ideology." The illusionary socialist "equality" not only did not work for the advantage of women, but also led to a reduction of women's concerns to empty slogans represented by the idea of the "women on the tractors" (Fuszara 2003). Indeed, the socialist solution did not go any deeper than the surface of empty slogans. Traditional women's roles as mothers (most powerfully embodied in the image of the Mother-Pole) and wives were never challenged (Brach-Czaina 1995, Walczewska 1999). Although, as indicated before, under Communism, women's participation in the labor force increased. The fact that such change was an effect of the imposition of the socialist regime from the outside made it unappreciated and unwanted. Furthermore, the understanding of work as mainly taking place within the sphere of production meant that reproductive work for which women were responsible, although important, was not seen as of equal status. Yet, the need for their labor on one hand, and the importance of preserving the nation on the other, required women to procreate.

Communism ridiculed "women's issues" in the eyes of women even more by banning free associations, and establishing and maintaining the pseudo-feminist, façade organizations across the region (e.g., The Polish Women's League, The Circles of Rural Housewives). These large-scale organizations, with million female members completely uncommitted to feminist program, perpetuated the myth of commitment to women through forced "equality," "statist feminism," and "women's emancipation" (Walczewska 1996). Fuszara argued that the meaningless character of communist emancipation became evident right after 1989 when the first free elections in Poland resulted in a drastic decrease of the percentage of women who were members of the national parliaments (Fuszara 2006).

The unprecedented growth of women's and feminist non-governmental organizations (NGOs) is just one of several indicators marking the arrival of the new gender regime after 1989. Many consider the year 1989 as a symbolic moment that signified the rebirth of the contemporary women's movement in Poland (Mizielińska 2009). By 2008, there were more than 300 active women's and feminist organizations, foundations, coalitions, associations, unions, and informal groups (e.g., eFKA, Konsola, Ulica Siostrzana (Street Sisterhood), March 8th Women's Agreement, Feminoteka, Lesbian Agreement, Mama Foundation, The Federation for Women and Family Planning, The Center for Women's Rights). These groups engage in addressing a wide-range of concerns locally, nationally, and to some degree also transnationally (e.g., The Network of East-West Women, Karat Coalition, ASTRA) by focusing on reproductive health and rights, labor market, trafficking of women, violence against women, and on an increase in women's political participation or promoting equal status—just to mention few areas. Many of these groups do not restrict their activities to one particular area, but instead work simultaneously on several topics. Although their transnational engagement is still limited, as Polish feminism rarely defines itself and relates its experiences to international and global context, women's and feminist actions nationally and internationally have achieved some spectacular successes (see the discussion of Alicja Tysiąc's case in the following text).

The shifting of the geopolitical position of Poland and Poland's admission to new international institutional structures such as the European Union (EU) drastically changed the context within which women's and feminist groups work and act. While groups themselves debate the strength of the influence of these changes on their identity and actions, one can argue that in fact their mobilizations and strategies were as much affected by the conservative and patriarchal State and Church as by the availability of the EU funding or the arrival of new norms, standards, and regulations.

continued

Despite the new internal and external context within which women's and feminist groups operate, these groups believe that much of their success is primarily a result of their agency's ability to develop new strategies, influence, negotiate, protest, challenge, and act within the new and reconfigured public space. They argue that the rapidly changing socio-economic and political circumstances produce new conditions and pressures that result in the need for new collaborations among the groups locally, nationally, and transnationally.

Some research does show, however, that Poland's membership in the EU has also played a significant role, although perhaps less recognized by women's and feminist groups, in the changing context within which these groups operate (Mizielińska; Regulska and Grabowska 2008). Mizielińska (2009) explicitly argues that the impact of the EU remains underestimated, although it has altered the ways through which women's NGOs not only collaborate, but also compete with each other.

Although Polish women have engaged in numerous struggles to secure their social, economic, and political rights, probably the most visible and long-standing efforts focus on securing their reproductive rights. Demonstrations, petitions, lobbying the parliament, engaging international organizations and mobilizing NGOs support, creating youth support groups, and distributing materials and contraceptives are only but few of the many strategies and activities in which Polish women's NGOs engaged to support women and publicize their struggle for the right to choose. Although the phrase *reproductive rights* does not exist in the Polish legal language, its several aspects (family planning, prenatal testing, and abortion) are subject to many Polish regulations and restrictions (Zielinska 2007, 9). The anti-abortion legislation, which was enacted on January 7, 1993, remains one of the most restrictive in Europe. The 15 years of its negative effects are widespread. The legal restrictions did not eliminate the cases of abortion; in fact, it forced it underground. Official statistics point to around 200 abortions done legally, but according to the Federation for Women and Family Planning, the numbers easily reach more than 100,000 and quite possibly are much larger (Nowicka 2007, 31).

Despite the availability of better medical care, the increase in miscarriages (more than 40,000 a year) reflects the scale at which abortions are performed underground, as well as the poor sanitary and health conditions in which they are performed (Nowicka 2007, 23). The drastically restricted access to abortion means that many women are forced to bear a child even though their health or life circumstances put them and their families in danger. The most well-known case was that of Alicja Tysiąc, a 35-year old woman, who despite being threatened with vision impairment and documented independent medical opinions from three doctors, was forced to have her third child. In 2003, Alicja Tysiąc, with the support of women's non-governmental organizations, took her case to the European Court of Human Rights. In February 2006, the case was heard, and in March 2008, the final judgment was passed. Tysiąc won her case. The European Court of Human Rights decided that Poland has violated Article 8 (the right to respect for private and family life) of the European Convention for the Protection of Human Rights and Fundamental Freedoms (Federation 2008). Poland was ordered to pay Tysiąc 25,000 Euros in damage.

Alicja Tysiąc's case is an excellent example of not only how Poland's membership in the EU has been successfully used by women's NGOs, but also points out the strength of a women's agency. It also shows how Polish women are capable of mobilizing diverse local, national, and transnational resources. Finally, it is an example of how Polish women's struggles are informed by women's mobilizations abroad (in Europe and the United States), as well as by the central and east European context within which they live and work.

References

Bator, J. 1999. Płeć demokracji. *Gazeta Wyborcza* 147, June 26.

Brach-Czaina, J. 1995. The problems of Polish feminism. *Kwartalnik Pedagogiczny* 1–2: 359–389.

De Beauvoir, Simone. 1972. *The second sex*. London, UK: Penguin Press.

eFKA. 2007. *Stulecie kobiet w parlamentach europejskich*. Krakow: Fundacja Kobeca.

Eisenstein, Hester. 1983. *Contemporary feminist thought: An assessment*. Boston: GK Hall.

Federation for Women and Family Planning. 2008. Retrieved at December 20, 2008 http://www.federa.org.pl/?page=static&static=20&lang=2.

Freedman, Estelle B. 2003. *No turning back: The history of feminism and the future of women*. New York: Ballantine Books.

Friedan, Betty. 1963. *The feminine mystique*. New York: Norton.

Fuszara, M. 2003. History of women's organizations. In Jacek Kurczewski et al. (eds.), *Civil society in Poland*. Warsaw: University of Warsaw.

Fuszara, M. 2006. *Kobiety w polityce*. Warsaw: Trio.

Gordon, Linda. 1994. *Pitied but not entitled: Single mothers and the history of welfare 1890–1935*. Cambridge, MA: Harvard University Press.

Graff, A. 2001. *Swiat bez Kobiet*. Warsaw: PAN.

Hanisch, Carol. 2006. *The Personal Is political: Second Wave and Beyond*. Retrieved on June 8, 2008, at http://scholar.alexanderstreet.com/pages/viewpage.action?pageId=2259.

Heywood, Leslie and Jennifer Drake. (eds.) 1997. *Third wave agenda. Being feminist, doing feminism*. Meanapolilis, MN: University of Minnesota Press.

Jacquette, J.S. 2003. Feminism and the challenges of the "Post-Cold War" world. *International Feminist Journal of Politics* 5(3): 331–354.

Lengermann, P.A., and Jill Niebrugge-Brantley. 1992. Contemporary feminist theory. In George Ritze (ed.), *Contemporary sociological theory*. New York: McGraw-Hill.

Lichtner, Daniel, McLaughlin, Diane K. and Ribar, David C. 1997. Welfare and the Rise in Female-Headed Families. *American Journal of Sociology*. 103(I): 112–143.

Lukić, J., J. Regulska, and D. Zaviršek. 2006. *Women and citizenship in Central and East Europe*. Surrey, UK: Ashgate Publisher.

McLanahan, Sara. 1985. Family structure and reproduction of poverty. *American Journal of Sociology* 90(4): 873–901.

Mizielińska, J. (2009). *Przyjaciółki czy rywalki? Wpływ Unii Europejskiej na relacje pomiędzy kobiecymi NGO-sami*. In M. Fuszara, M. Grabowska, J. Mizielińska, and J. Regulska (eds.), *Kooperacja czy Konflikt?: Państwo, Unia Europejska i Kobiety*. Warsaw: Wydawnictwa Akademickie i Profesjonalne.

NCCP. (2007). "New York: Demographics of Poor Children". National Center for Children in Poverty. Columbia University, Mailman School of Public Health. Retrieved at May 12, 2009, http://www.nccp.org.

Nowicka, W. 2007. Ustawa antyaborcyjna w Polsce. In *Prawa reprodukcyjne w Polsce: Skutki ustawy antyaborcyjnej*. Warsaw: Federecja na Rzecz Kobiet i Planowania Rodziny.

Pearce, Diana. 1978. Feminization of poverty: Women, work and welfare. *The Urban and Social Change Review* 11: 28–36.

Penn, S. 2005. *Solidarity's secret: The women who defeated communism in Poland*. Ann Arbor, MI: University of Michigan.

Pressman, Steven. 2003. Feminist explanation for the feminization of poverty. *Journal of Economic Issues* 37(2): 353–361.

Regulska, J., and M. Grabowska. 2008. Will it make a difference: EU enlargement and women's public discourse in Poland. In S. Roth (ed.), *Gender issues and women's movement in the European Union.* Oxford, UK: Berghahn Books.

Walczewska, S. 1996. Liga Kobiet. Jedyna orgnizacja kobieca w Polsce. *Pełnym Głosem* (1).

Watkins, Gloria J. 1984. *Feminist theory from margin to center.* Cambridge, MA: South End Press.

Zielinska, E. 2007. Przeglad polskich regulacji prawnych w zakresie praw reprodukcyjnych. In *Prawa reprodukcyjne w Polsce: Skutki ustawy antyaborcyjnej.* Warsaw: Federecja na Rzecz Kobiet i Planowania Rodziny.

Test Your Knowledge: Chapter 3

Short Answer Questions

1. Describe the change in women's life orientation in regards to their domestic and professional roles before and after 1960s in the United States. Brainstorm how this change most likely influences the societal roles of men.

2. Describe and compare the goals of the second and third wave of the feminist movements, and list the differences in men's and women's view on their social roles between the two waves.

3. In a comparative way, describe the goals and objectives of Western and post-colonial feminism.

Multiple-Choice Question

Instructions: Choose one answer to the following question.

The first feminist group was established in:

a. England
b. United States
c. France
d. Germany

Global Violence against Women

Definition of Violence against Women

Violence can be defined as the intentional use of physical force or power, threatened or actual, against oneself, another person, or against a group or community that either results in or has a high likelihood of resulting in injury, death, psychological harm, maldevelopment, or deprivation. It includes physical, sexual, and psychological abuse, such as the significant abuse of power arising from a dependent relationship, threats, intimidation, and neglect (World Health Organization 2008).

Violence against women is not a new concept and, despite it being historically rooted, broadly persists in the contemporary world. Deeply ingrained cultural norms and values promoting male dominance with domestic violence and, in some extreme cases, torture-like practices are greatly impacting the lives of billions of women today. Most societies across the world strictly defined what is "masculine" and "feminine" and with established gender roles, view masculine as desirable, whereas feminine is rejected. Within the framework of such belief, men are and were historically in control of societal life. They are considered to be the bread winners and decision makers, helping and providing for the family's well-being. At the same time, women are viewed as dispensable and expendable. In many societies, it is believed that the main benefit of girls in the family is to restore, carry on, and perpetuate family honor by remaining chaste and becoming an obedient child and partner in marriage. For this purpose, females remain under male control across their lifetime. Strict rules of conduct and guidelines of what women and girls can or cannot do are imposed on girls from early childhood.

Such attitudes lead to broadly spread violence against women, including the killing of unwanted infant girls (infanticide) or aborting a female fetus in late pregnancy to avoid the family burden of paying a dowry at the time of a girl's marriage. Among other forms of violence against women is wife beating. Many societies permit a husband to beat his wife. In some societies (e.g., contemporary Sri Lanka), domestic violence is so deeply ingrained in the culture that husbands routinely beat

their wives as a form of teaching future obedience and securing dominance. In such cultures, wives accept violence as a part of marital life.

The way that society talks about women and uses violence and force
against them has significant implications for women's life experiences
and for social policy. Cultural stereotypes about women and gender color
the way professionals in law enforcement, the legal system, the courts,
and social policy agencies treat women and perceive violent acts of
aggression committed against them. Gender stereotypes that continue to
permeate our society create the very cultural discourses that people in
positions of power and in the population at-large talk and perceive issues
of violence against women.

Thus, for example, the central component of the cultural system of
the United States is misogyny (hatred of women) and homophobia (irrational hatred of homosexuality). Both of these values lead to accelerated
violence against women, homosexuals, and bisexuals.

Manifestations of gender-related violence are closely determined by
national and global culture. In the United States, the most frequent forms
of violence against women are rape, domestic violence, and sexual harassment. Globally, the most frequent attention is devoted to problems of human trafficking, bride kidnapping, and female genital mutilation (FGM).

National Issues of Gendered Violence

Rape. Rape, is defined by the U.S. Department of Justice as forced
sexual intercourse. Forced sexual intercourse means vaginal, oral, or anal
penetration by offender(s). This category includes incidents where the penetration is from a foreign object such as a bottle. Certain types of rape under
this definition cannot cause pregnancy (U.S. Department of Justice 2005).

Rape is a frequently committed crime in the United States; every
two minutes someone is sexually assaulted. One out of every six American women has been the victim of an attempted or completed rape in a
lifetime (14.8 percent completed rape; 2.8 percent attempted rape) (U.S.
Department of Justice 2005). The United States has the world's highest
rape rate of the countries that publish such statistics. The rate is 4 times
higher than Germany, 13 times higher than England, and 20 times higher
than Japan. Additionally, 3 percent of American men, or 1 in 33, have
experienced an attempted or completed rape in a lifetime. In the United
States in 2003, 9 out of 10 rape victims were females, and 1 in every 10
rape victims was male. During their lifetime, 17.7 million of American
women and 2.78 million men have been victims of sexual assault or rape
(National Institute of Justice and Centers for Disease Control &
Prevention 1998).

Although about 80 percent of all victims are white, minorities are
somewhat more likely to be attacked. Statistics demonstrate that 17.7 percent of white women are victims of rape; 18.8 percent, black women; and
as many as 34.1 percent, Indian/Alaskan women. The victims of this
crime are not only adult women and men. Frequently, victims are children
(U.S. Department of Justice 2004). In fact, 15 percent of sexual assault and
rape victims are under age 12, with 93 percent of juvenile sexual assault
victims knowing their attackers, who are most often acquaintances (58.7
percent) or family members (34.2 percent) (Commonwealth 1998, U.S.
Department of Health & Human Services 1995).

Rape is a gendered crime with long-term consequences. The victims are 3 times more likely to suffer from depression, 6 times more likely to suffer from post-traumatic stress disorder, 13 times more likely to abuse alcohol, 26 times more likely to abuse drugs, and 4 times more likely to contemplate suicide (World Health Organization 2008). It is a crime surrounded by salience and shame of the abused person and thus not often reported. As some sources claim, only 16 percent of rape is reported to the police (CEASE 2008).

Sexual harassment. Sexual harassment is the second salient but frequently occurring problem of sexual violence in the United Stated. It is defined as unwelcome sexual advances or requests for sexual favors and other verbal or physical conduct of a sexual nature that is used against a victim of a lower social position and status than the offender. Sexual harassment takes place under conditions of a threat of using social, economic, or political power to destroy the harassed person if she or he does not submit to the request. The goal of this form of violence is intimidation, induction of fear, and limitation of progress or development of the harassed person.

To be classified as sexual harassment, the request for sexual favor or contacts must take place under the condition of an induced threat or denial of tenure, promotion, and other professional advancement if the requested favor is refused. Such refusal is used or expressed as it would be used against employment, professional progress, or educational progress of the harassed person. The refusal to submit to unwanted sexual conduct could also be used as a basis for academic decisions affecting individual educational achievement and personal development. Thus, the harassment has the purpose and effect of unreasonably interfering with an employee's work performance or student's academic performance. It creates an intimidating, hostile, and offensive working or learning environment (Komaromy et al. 1993).

The harassment could take various forms, but frequently it includes the creation of an offensive working or learning environment by repeated written, verbal, physical, and/or visual contact with sexual overtones. These overtones may be expressed in written or verbal form, including suggestive or obscene letters, notes, invitations; and derogatory comments, slurs, jokes, or epithets. Sexual harassment may also take physical forms, including assault, unwelcome touching, impeding or blocking movements, gestures, or display of sexually offensive objects and pictures. A classic example would be unnecessary touching, patting, hugging, or brushing against a person's body; remarks of a sexual nature about a person's clothing or body; remarks about sexual activity; or speculations about previous sexual experiences. Such behaviors lead to the establishment of a pattern of conduct in which the intimidated person feels humiliated and uncomfortable. Moreover, the sexual harassment continues after the offender is informed that the sexual interest is not welcomed.

Within the work environment, coercive sexual behavior is used to control, influence, and affect the employee's career, promotion, or salary. Coercive sexual behavior involves implying or actually withholding support for an appointment, promotion, or change of assignment; submitting or threatening to submit an undeserved performance report; and failing or threatening to fail the probationary period.

Within an academic environment, coercive sexual behavior is used to control, influence, or affect the educational opportunities, grades, or learning environment of a student, including withholding or threatening to withhold grades earned or deserved; submitting or threatening to submit an undeserved performance evaluation; and denying or threatening to deny a scholarship recommendation or college application.

Sexual violence is surrounded by salience, denial, and concealed knowledge, which leads to a lack of information about these crimes or lack of accurate information. Fallacies are reflected in circulated myths about sexual harrassment. For example, victims of sexual harassment are often believed to be only attractive women, whereas in reality every person is a potential victim. The crime is often believed to be rare and even welcomed by most victims. In reality, no person enjoys such sexual advances. These violent acts affect 7 out of every 10 women in American society, and the victims are predominantly women and rarely men.

Domestic violence. Lastly, domestic violence commonly occurs in American and other societies. Domestic violence and emotional abuse are behaviors used in a relationship by one person to control another person in a relationship. Partners may be married or not married; heterosexual, gay, or lesbian; and living together, separated, or dating. The classic examples of this crime include, but are not limited to, putdowns, keeping partners from contacts with friends and family members, withholding money from partners, and preventing the partner from getting or keeping a job. It includes physical harm or threat of harm, as well as sexual assault and public intimidation and stalking. The violence can be a serious criminal act, such as physical assault (hitting, pushing, shoving, etc.), sexual abuse (unwanted or forced sexual activity), and stalking. Although emotional, psychological, and financial abuses are not criminal behaviors, they are forms of abuse and can lead to criminal violence (Creative Communications Group 2009).

Contrary to past belief that victims of domestic violence are only poor, uneducated, and minority women, domestic violence can happened to anyone of any class. In the past, it was believed that alcohol, stress at work, and mental illness caused violence. However, research proved that, although these problems are frequently used as an excuse for violent acts, they are not the cause of crimes of violence. Generally, violent acts happen because the abuser has learned such behavior from others (frequently observing their own parents) and chooses to repeat it in their own relationship as a form of controlling a domestic partner (Michigan Judicial Institute 1998, 1–5).

Domestic violence usually does not start from severe sexual or physical assault (see Figure 4.1). In most cases, it begins slowly and over time builds to a circle of dependency, starting with creating a strong, emotional attachment of the victim to the abuser, followed by a slow, steady separation of the victim from her or his contacts and support of family members, friends, and other acquaintances. When the emotional ties and separation are being strengthened, the abuser separates the victim from her or his financial resources by controlling the finances or withholding monetary support, and preventing progress at work or future employment. Following the dependency and subordination, the episode of violent assault takes place, after which the abuser apologizes to induce self-blame on the victim. A period of calming down and making up for the aggression follows. After the first episode, the violence escalates, completing the cycle. Each cycle takes a different amount of time to complete, but it follows a circular pattern in which reoccurring episodes are characterized by increasingly more severe physical or/and sexual assaults and an increase of control. The cycle can happen hundreds of times in an abusive relationship. Each stage lasts a different amount of time in a relationship. The total cycle can take anywhere from a few hours to a year or more to complete. It is important to remember that not all relationships that include domestic violence fit the cycle. Often, as time goes on, the making up and calming stages disappear (Walker 1979).

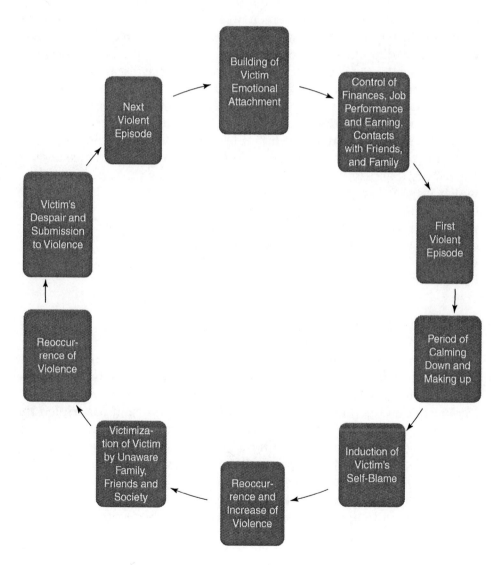

Figure 4.1 Circular notion of escalation of domestic violence over time

Source: Figure created by an author based on literary sources on process and principles of domestic violence (Berry 2000, Bancroft 2003, Walker 1979, Weiss 2004).

Similar to most cases of rape, domestic violence and sexual harassment are reoccurring crimes. They are crimes of control and demanded subordination; they are not sexual acts relating to the expression of love. They reflect the cultural frameworks of a particular society, especially prevailing gender roles, gender stereotypes, and behavioral norms. To change cultural behaviors and norms that are prone to violence against women, societies need to act together to form movements with anti-violence agendas.

One example of a society that formed an anti-violence movement occurred in 1979, in the small town of Maharashtra, India. When the high court reversed the conviction of a criminal who raped a 14-year-old girl, a public nationwide protest occurred, leading to an amendment of rape laws. Another example occurred in the United States when President Ronald Reagan withdrew funds from shelters. Reagan argued that it was a domestic issue. After national protests, the funds were returned. In Canada, the protective rape law shield for women, which protected the public display of sexual life history in courts, was taken back until after protests, a new law was re-instated, putting in place the shield. Since 1998, the Canadian government spends extensive funds on gendered violence research.

Like in other societies, some violent acts are accepted and supported in the United States. Football, for example, is about as violent as hand-to-hand combat and can cause spine injury and brain damage. However, football is a national ritual that upholds cultural values of competitiveness, toughness, and masculinity understood as male dominance and superiority (Sabo 2004). It is therefore not surprising that offenders of violence against women are not always brought to justice. On the contrary, victims are frequently victimized again by the justice system, police, and social norms. They are put to shame and blamed for experiencing violent acts. Protective laws are thus essential not only to limit violence against women and to protect victims, but also to change the behavioral expectation of male dominance.

Global Issues of Gendered Violence

Across the contemporary world, rapid social and economic changes have displaced many to urban centers and their outskirts, where people are powerless and without job security. Millions have become vulnerable to exploitation and slavery. The population explosion has tripled the amount of people in the world, with most growth taking place in the developing world. More frequently in developing than in developed countries, government corruption allows slavery, sexual exploitation, and other kinds of exploitation to go unpunished, even though it is illegal. Within this context, the third most profitable global form of organized crime, human trafficking and sex slavery, is spreading.

Human Trafficking and Sex Slavery. Human trafficking is a highly profitable crime, falling only behind the trafficking of drugs and arms. The human trafficking results from migration (legal and illegal) to well-developed countries in search of job opportunities. It is characterized by a lack of consent on the part of the trafficked person, and ongoing exploitation of the victims in some manner to generate illicit profits for the traffickers. In search for work, women and, in some cases, men are trapped or kidnapped to be sold as sex slaves and serve in the prostitution business. As soon as they enter the prostitution rings involuntarily (and in most cases forcefully), they are completely controlled by the brothel owner. Fearing arrest due to involvement in illegal prostitution and/or illegal status, as well as not being aware of their legal rights due to cultural and language barriers and deprivation of legal documents, victims are forced to stay in brothels as long as the owner wishes. In most cases, the victims are made to believe that the stay will end as soon as they pay off the debt of transporting to and securing a place to work. When the debt is paid off, however, the brothel owners may call the police and have the sex slave jailed. The price of a bribe to release the victim is very costly. After the brothel owner frees the sex slave, she or he returns to debt and continues to work for owner until the debt is paid off. A lack of a social network (families, friends, government) to fall back on, difficulty surviving on their own, and physical injury from severe violence (sometimes a sex slave's Achilles tendon is cut) perpetuates and makes the situation difficult to escape.

Other globally occurring violent acts like female genital mutilation (FGM), ritual scaring, or foot bonding that may be celebrated by family members as a step toward adulthood are discussed in length by Andrea Parrot (see box). In many countries, such acts uphold cultural values of female chastity and obedience and, although illegal in most countries and considered a crime against human rights by the United Nations, happen frequently across the world.

Some acts of violence against women are pertinent and determined by a culture of a particular country. One of such acts is bride kidnapping, which is spreading in post-communist Kyrgyz Republic. Bride kidnapping is the act of abducting a woman to marry. It includes a variety of actions, ranging from consensual marriage to kidnapping and rape. Typically, it involves a young man and his friends taking a young woman by force or deception to the home of his parents or a near relative. She is held in a room until his female relatives convince her to put on the marriage scarf. If necessary, she is kept overnight or raped, and is thus threatened by the shame of no longer being a pure woman. Studies show 80 to 90 percent of women stay in the men's house that abducted her.

Dr. Orunbaeva of Naryn helps to understand the custom of bride kidnapping (Kleinbach at al. 2005). She points out that a Kyrgyz girl grows up without experiencing force against her. Then for the first time, psychological, physical, and sexual force are used against her. After hours or days, she is tired, in shock, and not ready to use physical and moral force to resist a group of mostly older women. When she agrees, all relatives are notified, and a marriage celebration takes place in the following few days. The studies look at the percentage of Kyrgyz marriages that were the result of kidnappings and the percentage of these marriages that were non-consensual (against the will of the women). As Kleinbach and others have demonstrated, in the Kyrgyz Republic in the early 2000s, the frequency of kidnapping increased with the institution of democratic freedom (Kleinbach at al. 2005).

The democratic transition, with its introduction of personal freedom, stimulated a rebirth of an old, banned custom of bride kidnapping that was still formally banned but, being considered cultural practice, was tolerated. In this sense, the freedom was misinterpreted as lawlessness (Wejnert and Djumabaeva 2004).

Problems of global violence against women are embedded within the content of countries' culture pertaining to gender roles and norms. Therefore, proposed solutions and policies need to incorporate women's vulnerability to suppression and dominance stemming from culture and limited economic resources owned by women. Empowering women by improving their economic, political, and social status seems to be the fastest solution to improve women's quality of life and to combat violence against women.

Global Violence Against Women Across the Life Course

by Andrea Parrot, Ph.D.

INTRODUCTION

Violence against women (VAW) is a global social epidemic. The magnitude of suffering is incalculable, as are the long-term effects of so many women being beaten, raped, murdered, battered, and tortured (Parrot and Cummings 2008). This is not a new phenomenon, as it has been described as far back as the Bible (Parrot and Bechhofer 1991). It is actually pandemic and, although the types of violence vary from continent to continent, and culture to culture, almost every culture displays some type of violence against women. It is also a situation that affects girls and women throughout their lives. There is no time over the life course when girls or women do not experience violence, prenatal to old age. The only cultures where violence against women is not normative are the very few cultures that are matriarchal and matrilineal. The type of violence expressed in cultures is determined by the social and family structure that is normative in that culture, as well as history, cultural practices, and religion. World events, political unrest, and natural disasters also create circumstances that promote violence against women (such as sexual slavery, trafficking, rape as a war crime, etc).

Several violent practices aimed at women and girls are no longer legal, and have almost been eliminated entirely, but in general, VAW is increasing, rather than decreasing. Sati (self immolation by widows in India) and Chinese foot binding are two types of VAW that have almost been entirely eliminated. Legislation was passed to outlaw both of these practices, but legislation alone was not enough. Foot binding was declared illegal in 1911, but it continued to be practiced in rural areas until the Chinese Cultural Revolution (Cummings, Ling, and Stone 1997).

For strongly entrenched practices to change, cultural attitudes and norms must also change, or the consequences of violating the law must be so severe that people are forced to change.

Where girls and women are devalued, or seen as property of the father or the husband, they are often sold, beaten, forced into dangerous marriages, and even murdered. Several of the most common or most serious practices still occurring today that result in VAW are discussed below. These practices will be presented from a life course perspective, with those practices presented first that happen very early in a child's life, culminating with practices that happen at the end of a woman's life.

Prenatal and Early Childhood: Feticide and Infanticide

During the prenatal period, in many parts of South and East Asia boy babies are highly desired. And in China, where the *One Child Policy* is in effect, if a couple can have only one child, they frequently opt for a child of the preferred gender. As a result, the femicide of female fetuses is quite common, resulting in an imbalance of the sex ratio at birth such that there are as many as 116 males to 100 females born (Gittings 2002). The places where this practice is most common are parts of China, India, Pakistan, and South Korea (BBC 2008, Parrot and Cummings 2006). If a couple cannot find out the gender of the child through ultrasound which often results in the termination of the pregnancy if they are carrying a female fetus, then they sometimes resort to female infanticide, either through direct action or neglect. Prior to the advent to easy access to medical technologies (such as ultrasound, amniocentesis), infanticide was much more common. Although pregnancy termination based on gender alone, and infanticide are both illegal, the law has been quite ineffective in improving the sex ratio imbalance in those areas.

Childhood: Female Genital Mutilation, Sex Trafficking, Forced Marriage, Child Sexual Abuse

Female genital cutting, sometimes referred to as female genital mutilation (FGM) or female circumcision, is endured by approximately two million additional girls and women each year, primarily in regions of Africa and the Middle East (Cook, Dickens, and Fathalla 2002, Ellaithi et al. 2006). This practice is now found in many new areas of the world due to migration. It is usually done without anesthesia and often in unsanitary conditions, resulting in approximately 15 percent fatality as a result. In 2008, the death of a 10-year-old girl in Kenya resulting from FGM (Rosen 2008) received international attention, renewing the debate about FGM. Many argue that this is a case of cultural relativism and should be viewed simply as any other cultural practice, while human rights activists argue that FGM is a violation of fundamental human rights.

The trafficking of girls and women is a pandemic problem. As many as 800,000 are estimated to be trafficked each year (Lederer 2007). Most countries are either source countries, transit countries, or destination countries—sometimes all three. Traffickers obtain girls and women through kidnapping, buying, manipulating, or lying to girls to send them to slavery and torture, frequently sexual exploitation, often resulting in death from AIDS. While many women succumb to this fate, children are being increasingly sought by sex traffickers because they are less likely to have contracted sexually transmitted diseases. Even if these girls and women are rescued or escape, they are often physically and/or emotionally scarred for life. Girls who are not trafficked are still at risk for child sexual abuse, which is experienced by as many as one out of four girls in many developed nations (including the United States) encounter. This abuse often is traumatic, physically and mentally, and frequently is ongoing for many years.

In some parts of Asia, Africa, and the Middle East primarily, girls and women often enter into marriage through an arrangement by their parents. If the brides are willing, this can be a happy and fulfilling arrangement. However, sometimes women, and even young girls, are forced into marriages they do not want, which sometimes results in repeated rapes and battering. In Afghanistan, for example, as economic hardship increases, selling brides becomes more common, and UNICEF (2005) estimates that between 60 to 80 percent of marriages there are forced.

Teenage—Adulthood: Rape in War, Bride Kidnapping, Domestic Violence, Sexual Assault, Honor Killing, Sexual Slavery, and Acid Attacks

Throughout history, women have been raped as "spoils of war." However, rape has been used as a war crime with different motivations and outcomes in the recent wars, most notably in Africa and Europe. As atrocious as rape in war has been historically, in the recent past women have been gang raped and impregnated as a means of "ethnic cleansing." Women are also being gang raped to infect them with HIV so that they

Continued

will not only become ill themselves, but they will also become vectors of disease that they may continue to spread long after the war ends.

In several countries primarily in Central Asia, most commonly Kyrgyzstan, Kazakhstan, Pakistan, Bangladesh, India, Ethiopia, and Uzbekistan, bride kidnapping occurs with regularity (Parrot and Cummings 2008). When the bride and groom both desire this, it is not a form of VAW. However, in many cases, it is a cultural practice used by men to obtain a bride against her will and without her consent. In some cases, the "bride" has never even met the man, but he fancies her. In the non-consensual cases, force and coercion are used to obtain the woman and to get her to "agree to the marriage." Rape is also employed to sully the woman's reputation so that even if she does not want to stay, once she is no longer a virgin, she will likely be rejected by any other man as a wife. In Kyrgyzstan, approximately 35 to 45 percent of women have been married against their will (Kleinbach, Ablezova, and Aitieva 2005).

In industrialized nations intimate partner violence and sexual assault are the most common forms of violence against women, but these types of violence also occur in the Global South. With the migration of people from parts of the world where specific types of VAW are common, heretofore uncommon harmful practices are occurring with greater regularity in developed nations. The Centers for Disease Control (2002) estimate that more than 1.5 million women are victims of intimate partner violence each year.

In several countries in South East Asia, most notably India, dowry deaths and bride burning occur as a result of the Dowry system, and a cultural expectation that all women must be married (Panchanandeswaran and Koverola 2005). Although Dowry has been illegal since the passage of the Dowry Prohibition Act in 1961, it is still quite common, and often expected for a family to make a "good" match for their daughter. If the bride's family is not able to pay a sufficient dowry, or is unable to meet continuing demands for additional dowry, the result may be an "accidental kitchen fire" in which the bride is seriously burned, often fatally (Oldenburg 2002). There are many other ways in which brides are killed in dowry disputes, but burning her to death is the most common.

Honor killings (sometimes called "crimes of passion") are reported regularly in many different parts of the world: Africa, the Middle East, Europe, Asia, and Latin America primarily (Mayell 2002). These are usually murders of women by the men in their families if the woman was proven or believed to have had sex outside of marriage. Sometimes, this crime occurs if a woman chooses her own husband and elopes, without the family's permission. The men who commit these murders are often viewed as heroes for "restoring the family's honor." And offenders have traditionally been treated very leniently by the courts if the murder was a crime of passion, or if the family sends a minor to "restore the family's honor."

Sexual slavery can happen in many contexts: via sex trafficking, in prison, in marriage, through forced marriages, with religious motivation, or via debt bondage. There are several forms of ritual sexual slavery that are religiously endorsed: in West Africa (Trokosi) and India (Devedasi). As of 2001, as many as 10,000 girls and women were serving as Torkosi sex slaves (Boaten 2001). In the case of both Trokosi and Devedasi, young, disenfranchised women or girls, typically from poor families, are given or sold to religious leaders for servitude. Part of the servitude is sexual. "Temple prostitution (Devedasi), practiced by Dalits (Untouchables) on their women and girls, is violence sanctioned by religion" (Grey 2005, 139).

Acid attacks on women are increasing in some parts of Asia, most notably India, Pakistan, Bangladesh, Cambodia, and Burma. The motivation for these attacks is often sexual in nature, especially if a woman has rejected a male suitor; however, there are other motivations as well. Most victims are young and female (Lawson 2002). The acid, usually easy-to-obtain battery acid, is thrown over the woman's head, face, and neck, permanently disfiguring her, sometimes blinding her, and causing a great deal of pain. If the attack was motivated by sexual or romantic rejection, the attacker will likely disfigure her so drastically that no other man will ever want her.

Old Age: Widow Abuse, Sati

Although Sati is very rare today, mistreatment of widows in some parts of India still occurs. Widows in India still routinely experience humiliations, hardships, and extreme ostracism (Girish 2004). It was only about 150 years ago that it was actually illegal for widows in India to remarry, prior to the passage of the Widow Remarriage Act in 1856. After a woman becomes a widow, no matter her age, she is forced to give up her bridal jewelry; her head is shaved and her body is wrapped in a stark white sari so she may not arouse other men sexually (Girish 2004). She is considered bad luck, and is often thrown out by her in-laws. She may be forced to beg or sell her body for sex to survive.

Conclusion

Although the regions mentioned above are associated with a specific type of violence, that type of violence is not limited to only those regions or cultures. In addition, while these practices do or have occurred within that region or culture, not all the people in those communities actually do engage in or condone such practices. Because of migration, many types of violence against women that were limited to one region have begun to occur in places where they were not practiced. And while some practices were traditionally associated with a particular religion, they have expanded to other religions as well if they became part of the culture and thereby pervasive within the entire community.

"Because of the overwhelming numbers of women who are sexually exploited on a daily basis, legislative changes are inevitably limited in their ability to significantly affect this global issue." (Parrot and Cummings 2008, xiii). Until men no longer believe that they have a right to use women's bodies for profit, exploitation, and their own pleasure, attempts to address these practices will have limited success. The root causes of VAW that support the continued subordination of women must be challenged as well, such as racism, colonialism, economic deprivation, and global economies that exclude certain oppressed groups (MacKinnon 2005).

- Building of Victim Emotional Attachment
- Control and Domination of the Relationship in terms of Finances, Job Performance and Earning, Contacts with Friends and Family members
- First Violent Episode
- Induction of Victim's Self-Blame
- Reoccurrence and Increase of Violence
- Victimization of Victim by Unaware Family, Friends, and Society
- Reoccurrence of Violence
- Victim's Despair and Submission to Violence

References

Bancroft, Lundy. 2003. *Why does he do that?* New York: Berkley Books.

BBC. 2008. Female infanticide. *Religion and Ethics*. Retrieved September 20, 2008, at http://www.bbc.co.uk/ethics/abortion/medical/infanticide_1.shtml.

Berry, Dawn. 2000. *Domestic violence*. New York: McGraw-Hill.

Boaten, A.B. 2001. The trokosi system in Ghana: Discrimination against women and children. In A. Rwomire (ed.), *African women and children: Crisis and response*. Westport, CT: Praeger Publishers.

CEASE. 2008. Coalition Educating about Sexual Endangerment. Ohio State University. Retrieved on April 20, 2009, at http://oak.cats.ohiou.edu/~ad361896/anne/cease/rapestatisticspage.html.

Commonwealth. 1998. *Commonwealth fund survey of the health of adolescent girls.*

Creative Communications Group. 2007. Domestic violence should not happen to anybody . . . ever . . . period! Oakland County Coordinating Council Against Domestic Violence. Retrieved on May 27, 2009, at www.jmir.org/2003/4/e25/HTML

Cummings, S.R., X. Ling, and K. Stone. 1997. Consequences of foot binding among older women in Beijing, China. *American Journal of Public Health 87*(10): 1677–1679.

Ellaithi, M., T. Nilsson, D. Gisselsson, A. Elagib, H. Eltigani, and I. Fadl-Elmula. 2006. Female genital mutilation of a karyotypic male presenting as a female with delayed puberty. *BMC Women's Health 6* (6). Retrieved on September 10, 2008, at http://www.biomedcentral.com/1472-6874/6/6.

Girish, U. 2004. India's outcast widows have new havens. *Women's E-news.* Retrieved on September 15, 2008, at http://www.womensenews.org/article.cfm/dyn/aid/1794/.

Gittings, J. 2002. Sex imbalance shocks China. *The Guardian.* Retrieved on September 1, 2008, at http://www.guardian.co.uk/world/2002/may/13/gender.china.

Grey, M. 2005. Dalit women and the struggle for justice in a world of global capitalism. *Feminist Theology 14(1)*: 127–149.

Kleinbach, R., M. Ablezova, and M. Aitieva. 2005. Kidnapping for marriage (Ala Kachuu) in a Kyrgyz village. *Central Asian Survey* 24(2): 191–202.

Komaromy Miriam, Andrew Bindman, Richard Haber, and Merle Sande. 1993. Sexual harassment in medical training. *The New England Journal of Medicine* 328: 322–326.

Lawson, A. 2002. Bangladesh protects against acid attacks. *BBC News.* Retrieved on September 15, 2008, at http://news.bbc.co.uk/2/hi/south_asia/1861157.stm.

Lederer, L. 2007. In modern bondage: An international perspective on human trafficking in the 21st century. Remarks at the Federal Acquisition Regulation Compliance Training for Government Contractors, Washington D.C. Retrieved on January 12, 2008, at http://www.state.gov/g/tip/rls/rm/07/96276.html.

Mackinnon, C. 2005. Pornography as trafficking. *Michigan Journal of International Law 26*: 993–1012.

Michigan Judicial Institute. 1998. *Domestic violence benchbook*, pp. 1–5.

National Institute of Justice and Centers for Disease Control & Prevention. 1998. *Prevalence, incidence and consequences of violence against women survey.*

Oldenburg, V.T. 2002. *Dowry murder: The imperial origins of a cultural crime.* Oxford UK: Oxford University Press.

Panchanandeswaran, S., and C. Koverola. 2005. The voices of battered women in India. *Violence Against Women 11*(6): 736–758.

Parrot, Andrea and Laurie Bechhofer. 1991. *Acquaintance rape: The hidden crime.* New York: John Wiley and Sons.

Parrot, Andrea and Nina Cummings. 2006. *Forsaken females: The global brutalization of women.* New York: Rowman and Littlefield.

_____. 2008. *Sexual enslavement of girls and women worldwide.* London: Praeger.

Rosen, K. 2008. Ten year old girl dies from FGM, Circumciser arrested. *V-Day 1.* Retrieved on September 15, 2008, at http://v10.vday.org/news-alerts/cry-of-a-girl.

Sabo, Don. 2004. Masculinities and men's health: Moving toward post-superman era prevention. In M. Kimmel and M. Messner (eds.), *Men's lives.* Boston: Allyn & Bacon.

United Nations Children's Fund (UNICEF). 2005. *Early marriage: a harmful traditional practice.*

U.S. Department of Health & Human Services. 1995. *Child maltreatment survey.* U.S. Administration for Children and Families.

U.S. Department of Justice. 2004. *National crime victimization survey.* Washington, DC.
_____. 2005. *National crime victimization survey.* Washington, DC.

Walker, Lenore. 1979. *The battered woman.* New York: Harper and Row.

Weiss, Elaine. 2004. *Surviving domestic violence: Voices of women who broke free.* New York: Volcano Press.

Wejnert, Barbara and Alma Djumabaeva. 2004. From patriarchy to egalitarianism: Parenting roles in democratizing Poland and Kyrgyzstan. *Marriage and Family Review* 3-4: 147–171.

World Health Organization. 2008. *Violence against women.* Retrieved on May 28, 2009, at www.who.int/mediacentre/factsheets/fs239.

Name_____

Test Your Knowledge: Chapter 4

Essay Questions

1. Define global gender violence using a functionalist perspective. Provide a description, examples, and a justification of the statement that gender violence is global.

2. Using the concept of the cycle of domestic violence, explain why victims of domestic violence frequently return to abusive spouses.

5

Global Development and Women at Work

Broadly spread violence against women could be prevented if women had higher social status and position in every country. Researchers have shown that women's societal position and social status closely relate to their earning abilities (Amott and Mattaei 1996, Coleman 2004). In any country, women's status is also circumscribed by underlying social, legal, political, economic, and cultural characteristics of the particular country. Thus, the achievement of a higher status by women should directly relate to gender equality at work, defined by women representation in the labor force and their equality of earning capacity (both of which are submerged within the particular culture), and the political and socio-economic characteristics of a country, as well as the processes of global development.

Whether economic development extends or restricts women's economic opportunities and status is presented in the next section of this chapter.

Global Development and Women Labor Force

Over the last several years, scholars are indicating that configurations of gender are deeply dependent on geo-political demarcations (Funk and Mueller 1993, Mohanty 2006, Rueschemeyer 1998, Wejnert and Djumabaeva 2003). Stemming from this research are concerns related to equality of women in the labor force. One concern is the **feminization of labor**. The phrase *feminization of labor* has been developed to refer to the global, competitive, export-oriented economies of countries that heavily rely on women's work. It has been hypothesized that the increasing globalization of production, the pursuit of flexible forms of labor to retain or increase competitiveness, and the changing job structures in industrial enterprises favor the feminization of employment. Women have been able to enter various types of jobs and rapidly increase their labor force participation regardless of the context of declined value of labor and growing unemployment (see Figure 5.1).

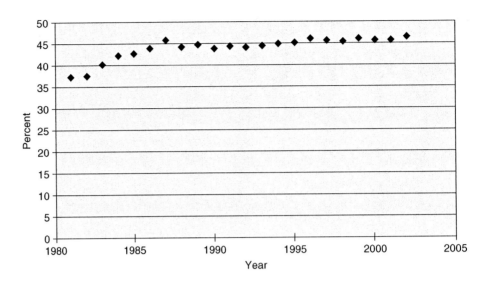

Figure 5.1 Change in trend of women labor force participation in the rapidly developing globalized economy in Taiwan

Source: Adapted from Directorate-General of Budget, Accounting and Statistics, Executive Yuan, ROC, *Yearbook of Labor Statistics, Taiwan Area, Republic of China*, various years.

Women labor market participation, however, has been accompanied by the deterioration of working conditions (labor standards, income, and employment status). Moreover, women labor market participation has not been accompanied by a redistribution of domestic, household, and child-care responsibilities. Disproportionately, women are involved in forms of employment that are used to maximize profits (temporary, part-time, seasonal, and home-based work). Some studies use this fact to examine the deterioration of working conditions for women (Standing 1989).

The process of feminization of labor continues in the manufacturing sector and in public services. Since the 1990s, throughout the world public sector, wages and industrial wages have been declining, but women's labor participation has grown by at least 10 percent during that time (Moghadam 2000). Employers preferred women workers because of their "nimble fingers" and capacity of hard work for low wages (Heyzer 1986; Lim 1985). Employers believed that women were more "docile" and less likely than men to rebel against monotonous, repetitive work and harsh working conditions (Elson and Pearson 1981).

In fast-developing economies, the primary industry shifted from manufacturing sector to service sector by the 1990s, and more women entered white-collar jobs in finance and insurance, real estate and rental, educational services, health care and social welfare, and public administration. Women holding these professional jobs received higher wages and were able to move out of the feminized labor category.

Scholars analyzing the impact of global development and countries cultural, socio-economic, and political characteristics on women's employment have argued that more attention should be paid not only to the impact of globalization on women's employment, but also to women's work outside the job market in the invisible economy of household and in the informal sector (usually defined as a sector outside the purview of the state and social security) (Beneria 2003, Ehrenreich and

Hochschild, 2003, Moghadam 2000, Schaeffer 2003). Unregistered small-scale urban enterprises, domestic servant work, housework, and self-employment may fall into this category, which involves subcontracting and home-based work.

As many studies have shown, women in the informal sector earn lower wages than in the formal sector, with no consistency in work contracts, difficult working conditions, and long working hours (Balakrishnan and Huang 2000, Beneria 2003). Many women accept this kind of work as a convenient form of income generation because it allows them to carry out domestic responsibilities and care for children. As a result, employment in the informal sector requires gender perspective to understand employers' use of "flexible" and "cheaper" female labor to increase profit and remain competitive on domestic and international market.

Although informal sector jobs share some characteristics, such as uncertain work environments, no standardized work content, and low job stability, their differences should not be ignored. For example, in the informal sector in Taiwan, women are not homogeneously unskilled, poor, and inferior compared to formal sector employees in terms of educational level, work experience, and earnings (Yu 2001). Self-employed and family enterprise workers possess capital comparable to formal sector employees in private enterprises, and self-employed women may even have more social capital (i.e., social networks that enhance business performance) and receive higher earnings than formal sector employees (Yu 2001).

In contrast, home-based pieceworkers match the stereotype of the informal sector in both qualifications and earnings. These types of jobs are performed by women in urban, industrial centers and agricultural areas across the developing world (Vagneron 2000).

Gender Wage Gap and Global Development

Under rapid growth and absorption of labor into labor-intensive export-oriented manufacturing, women have experienced a wage increase as their share of industrial employment has expanded. However, researchers argue that large gender wage differentials have been a stimulus to export growth and to freeing direct investment (Barendt and Bettina 2005, Garrett 2004, Hutton and Giddens 2000). Low female wages served as an incentive for foreign investment and an increase of exports in developing countries. Lowering labor costs per unit of produced goods increased gained capital of foreign investors from produced abroad goods and encouraged other investors to open manufacturing, which stimulates growth rates in economically developing countries (Seguino 2000). That is, the gender wage gap can partly explain the rapid economic growth of some countries (e.g., Asian South East countries).

The International Labor Organization's data show that, in the United States, female earnings lagged behind male earnings in all occupations for which comparative data are available, and that the gap increased from 1990 to 2000 in all occupations except computer programming (ILO 2005). The largest differential was in accounting, where females earned on average only three-quarters of what males in the same occupation earned. Even in the more female-dominated occupations of nursing and teaching, males continued to earn more than females. Overall, data on the 1992 annual report indicated that women earned about 70 percent of men's wage (U.S. Bureau of the Census 1993). Data on Scandinavian countries, which provide the most women-friendly social welfare, show that the gender wage gap has gradually been decreased. Women in those countries have earned about 90 percent of men's wage.

According to Petersen and Morgan (2001), the gender wage gap can be attributed to a variety of factors. Among them are **supply factors**, which include differences in quantities of labor competing for job slots and labor productivity, and **institutional factors** containing gender norms and social stereotypes that influence occupational segregation. Also **state-level policies** structured according to gender differences that influence differential distribution of resources enhanced differences in women as compared to men salaries and wages. Lastly, low wages of women depended on labor competition called **labor demand factor**. This factor was determined by the large number of women seeking employment opportunities in the rapidly growing, low-skilled manufacturing sector opened by foreign investors in post-colonial countries and developing countries that welcome a global market economy. Consequently, countries' economic growth, job performance, and job competition are among stimulants that encourage lower wages for women.

Why in the new global market economy of the contemporary global world, are women subject to an earning gap, feminization of manufacturing labor, and forced to take unpaid or underpaid domestic service jobs (nanny, maid, and caregiver to elderly)? As discussed in the beginning of the chapter, many authors revealed that the low value and payment for women labor is perpetuated because it increases the economic growth of countries (Barendt and Bettina 2005, Seguino 2000). Some authors, however, argue that it is also determined by prevalent gender stereotypes existing within each country.

According to Petersen and Morgan (2001), the gender wage gap can be attributed to a variety of factors. Among them are **supply factors**, which include differences in quantities of labor competing for job slots and labor productivity. **Institutional factors** are gender norms and social stereotypes that influence occupational segregation, which is defined as the division of work on women-type (low salaries, low skilled, repetitive, tedious with prolonged hours) and male-type (higher salaries, interesting, requiring higher skills). **State-level policies** are structured according to gender differences that influence differential distribution of resources. **Labor demand factors** affect economy growth and job performance.

The institutional factors alone explain about 40 percent of the wage gap, whereas all other studied factors (supply, state-level, and labor demand) account for the next 40 percent of the remaining wage gap. Hence, the cultural gender norms overpowered political (state-level policies) and economic (economy growth, labor productivity) influences (Petersen and Morgan 2001). Some scholars argue that the negative effect of gender stereotypes intensifies during economic instability, growing unemployment, and economic crises, and is determined by a state's need to lower unemployment level and provide security of work placement for male workers (Wejnert 2003)

A discussion on the impact and power of gender stereotype on women inequality on the labor market of rapidly economically developing Poland is presented in the box.

Media Generated Stereotypes of Polish Women Before and After the Transition to a Global Market Economy

by Elzbieta Sawa-Czajka

In the 1970s, information about the major feminist movements around the world reached Polish newspapers, which had become concerned with socio-political and cultural issues for the first time. Information about this topic often negatively constructed women's stereotypes, their social functions, and needs. Authors characterized the American women's liberation movement flippantly, stating that, "it is increasingly difficult to treat the women's movement as a joke, but to take it seriously is not easy . . . " (Krasicki 1972, 3). In the United States, the extent to which the level of toleration for mockery was breached forced the government to seriously discuss the concerns of prominent women's organizations. The agenda of women's organizations could not be discussed in any case however in Poland, as organizations were controlled by the state rather than independently. At that time, Polish women could at most belong to the League of Women or Societies of Village Women, and theoretically enjoy the equal opportunities the communist system provided for them. Journalists behind the Iron Curtain perceived the women who held positions such as the Vice-President in U.S. universities as merely a harmless eccentricity. Professor Ewa Kagan-Kans, a Polish journalist, expressed surprise when he heard that women held powerful positions in academia and stated authoritatively in an interview that, "the Polish reader does not treat the women's lib movement too seriously. He treats the question of whether women are less capable than men as largely as largely rhetorical (Wroblewski 1972)."

In 1980–1981 when the breakthrough Solidarity strikes highlighted the scale of economic and social problems, the social consequences were born mostly for women. There was then a new model for a woman: activist and striker during the Solidarity movement and a conspirator and conspirator's wife during the subsequent martial law (Penn 2005). It is these brave women that did not break down during the investigations. They had the courage to publicly oppose the government, comment on situations in Poland for free radios (Dr. Barbara Labuda from Wroclaw) and they provide support for conspiracy men[1]. Some of them were included with governing bodies of Seym and Senate after the 1989 changes. Typically, women were not involved in lobbying and power struggles within parties. They were more pragmatic and willing to compromise than their male counterparts working in the party system. In those 90-years in the Seym and the Senate a Parliamentary Group of Women acted over the political divisions that attempted to promote the rights of women in Parliament. It is also important to recall that one of the most popular politicians of the 90-years was Prof. Ewa Łętowska, who was the first Ombudsman in Poland.

In Poland in the 1990s, information about Polish feminist movements and organizations was frequently included in newspaper publication. Polish feminists were charac-

---

[1]These attitudes were reflected in literature and film, for instance J. Kuroń, *Wiara i wina*, Warszawa 1990; L. Wałęsa, *Droga nadziei*, Warszawa 1990; Z. Bujak, *Przepraszam za Solidarność*, Warszawa 1992; M. Nurowska, *Panny i wdowy*, Warszawa 1992; and also films, Człowiek z marmuru and Człowiek z żelaza; also the magazine article *Opowiem ci o Sierpniu*, Twój styl, nr 8/2005.

Continued

terized as young, educated, and usually in permanent relationships with male partners or spouses. The core agenda of the Polish feminist movement included the right to abortion, or the woman's right to choose; quality of life issues in both the work and domestic sphere, professional discrimination of women in work places, and also an increase of women participation in political and decision making institutions.

Another group of women that began to be visibly represented in Polish society was businesswomen, notably women who were running their own companies after 1990. In Poland, the image of the businesswomen currently promoted by the press is a vigorous, hard working female, who is a good negotiator, and very successful. At the same time, however, the image of woman as family care-giver and mother was still prominent. In interviews with businesswomen, it was frequently emphasized that the most important concerns for these women were still their children, maintaining a successful marriage and, in extreme cases, they also apologized for their professional successes. It is hard to believe that in such conditions women could have achieved such success while simultaneously juggling an intensive professional work schedule and the responsibilities of the ideal mother-homemaker. The primary duty of women at home was perpetuated by the dominant stereotypical media image in 1970s and 1980s when media presented Polish woman as a domesticated, submissive, multifunctional robot designed solely for child-rearing, homemaker and hostess. As Jerzy Urban writes "The idea of full time employment will be difficult to reconcile with the principle of cost-effective employment, technological progress and productivity growth. It will be enough . . . just in secret accept the principle that full employment applies only to the male population - and it already can be reconciled to some extent the contradictory desire to be fully employed, yet not excessively" (Urban 1972, 3).

The Martyrdom model of Polish Mother was engrained in women so deeply that there were unable to reject it verbally or publically, and media frequently permutated the traditional model of Polish mother. For instance, in the early years of 1990s writing about women highlighted the connected of a wife's interests directly to the interests of her husband. Accordingly, *Sukces* magazine wrote that it is the husband who must agree to whether his wife will establish and begin to work in her own company. *Sukces* writes about an owner of a large company in these words: "She fulfils a very responsible function thanks to her own husband, who, far from accepting the idea (!), agreed to her provision of familial financial support—and even "transferred to the wife the responsibility of being the President of the company she established. Although she is a Polish businesswoman managing a company just as well as any man, she still confesses that she does not put her successful career before her marriage and children" (Obrębka 1994, 5).

Stereotypes of masculinity and femininity are further shaped by the school textbooks as well, especially in classes for younger students. In reading primers and first reading texts, the mother is usually reduced to performing cooking duties for the family and is immersed with pots, pans and purchases. The mother and daughter prepare meals while dad and brother read, discuss, and help the sister and daughter in math (the authors of textbook evidently ignorant to the fact that among Polish researchers only Maria Skłodowska-Curie was twice the Nobel Prize laureate) (Bober and Brandt-Konopka 1994). Perhaps this phenomenon could be explained if the authors of the primers were men, but the vast majority is indeed women, thus making the situation perplexing to the educated woman.

Another stereotype being presented through advertising is the Polish woman who uses Dove soap, drinks Jacobs coffee, and "if she wants to be trendy and modern"- she purchases cosmetics guaranteed by the Laboratoire Garnier Paris. These women were the housewives extolling the benefits of detergents, and even writing letters to the washing powders as if these matters were their utmost concern. Polish women were treated for 90-years by marketing agencies (especially in television commercials) as silly and simple creatures who buy everything that is nicely packaged.

Many women's magazines during these same 90-years documented interviews with women of different professions, interests, achievements and ways of life. They were usually bargaining with a desire to convince the reader that the women interviewed were upper-class socialites who, if not brought up in the mansion, or even in the palace, at least had connections extending to the finest mansions in Europe. These Ladies usually lost private land and estates in the former Eastern parts of Poland that, after World War II, were incorporated as part of the Soviet Union. At home they cultivated traditional customs and at least one of their children lived abroad. Titles of the interviews, such as "Lady of Podlasie" and "Lady in purple," indicate who these Ladies are, or supposed to be.

The harsh realities of women the 1990's Poland paints a drastically different picture Women's unemployment climbed to 50 percent and the rate was increasing steadily. The media certainly helped generate a discriminatory environment. Gender stereotyping was rampant in advertisement for available jobs published in national newspapers. On ad explicitly included assumptions about the traditional patriarchal division of labor, stating, it was "seeking a man for the post of director (president, chief accounting officer) and a woman for the post of secretary, below 25 years-old." (Rzeczpospolita 1995).

At first, the Polish feminist movement did not notice and did not protest against that type of discriminatory advertising. But by mid-1995, small feminist groups began to formally oppose politicians and journalists' statements humiliating the value of women's work. Soon thereafter strong public reactions lashed back against feminist protesters. The frustrated male scientist and writer Waldemar Lysiak, went so far as to compare feminism to the "mentality of whores" (Łysiak 1994, 45).

During the first years of transition to the global market economy the lack of protests from women about their needs strengthened and reinforced negative assumptions surrounding gender. Generally, stereotypical images characterized the male as organized, logical, and strong while the female was imagined to be disheveled, irrational, and weak both mentally and physically in relation to men. It was not until the early 2000's when the stereotype of the Polish woman as the tired, bitter, and frustrated mother was replaced by a positive one where Polish women were portrayed as individuals involved in changing their own lives, controlling their own destinies and expressing their personal needs and desires. The change from the traditional and ubiquitous mother homemaker to that of a multi-faceted individual was decisively correlated with the progresses and perseverance of established groups and organizations working on behalf of women's issues and interests. Undoubtedly, the development and diffusion of communication and information technologies, particularly the Internet, helped to expand and empower the idea of womanhood in the Polish imagination. Mainly through the use of an internet, women's organizations were able to find support and information about feminist movements in other countries.

A recent initiative in Poland has been the establishment of a women's political party, proudly called the Women's Party, which was founded by Manuela Gretkowska. Although it is too early to assess the effectiveness of these actions, judging by its agenda and objectives, there is hope that soon there will be a new party to help enhance, secure and recognize the rights Polish women have fought for and deserve (Polska jest Kobieta 2007).

References

Amott, Teresa, and Julie Matthaei. 1996. *Race, gender and work.* Boston: South End Press.

Balakrishnan, R., and M. Huang. 2000. *Flexible workers—hidden employers: Gender and subcontracting in the global economy.* Report on a research project of women's economic and legal rights program. Washington, DC: The Asia Foundation.

Barendt, Regina, and Bettina Musiolek. 2005. *Workers' voices: The situation of women in the eastern European and Turkish garment industries.* Geneva: Human Rights at Work Foundation.

Beneria, L. 2003. *Gender, development, and globalization: Economics as if all people mattered.* London: Routledge.

Bober, E., and M. Brandt-Konopka. 1994. *A textbook to learn writing and reading.* Gdańsk, Poland: Wydawnictwo Gdansk.

Bujak, Zbigniew. 1992. *Przepraszam za Solidarność.* PWN: Warsaw.

Coleman, Isobel. 2004. The payoff from women's rights. Review paper. *Foreign Affairs,* March.

Ehreneich, Barbara, and Arlie Russell Hochschild. 2003. *Global woman: Nannies, maids, and sex workers in the new economy.* New York: Macmillan.

Elson, D., and R. Pearson. 1981. Nimble fingers make cheap workers: An analysis of women's employment in third world export manufacturing. *Feminist Review* (Spring): 87–107.

Funk, Nanette, and Magda Mueller. 1993. *Gender politics and post-communism.* New York: Routledge.

Garrett, Geoffrey. 2004. Globalization's missing middle. *Foreign Affairs* (November/December): 84–96.

Heyzer, N. 1986. *Working women in southeast Asia.* London: Open University Press.

Hutton, Will, and Anthony Giddens. 2000. *On the edge: Living with global capitalism.* London: Jonathan Cape.

Industrial Labor Organization. 2005. Women work more, but are still paid less. Retrieved on May 20, 2009, at www.ilo.org/global/About_the_ILO/Media _and_public_information/Press_releases/lang—en/WCMS_008091/ index.htm.

Krasicki, M. 1972. White tango. *Polityka* 32: 5, August 5.

Kuroń, Jacek. 1990. *Wiara i wina.* PAN: Warsaw.

Lim, L. 1985. *Women workers in multinational enterprises in developing countries.* Geneva: International Labor Organization.

Lu, Y. 2001. The "boss's wife" and Taiwanese small family business. In M.C. Brinton (ed.), *Women's working lives in East Asia.* Standford, CA: Standford University Press.

Łysiak, Waldemar. 1994. Brak wstydu. *Wprost* 47: 45, November 20.

Moghadam, V.M. 2000. Gender and the global economy. In M.M. Ferree, J. Lorber, and B.B. Hess (eds.), *Revisioning gender.* Lanham, MD: Rowman & Littlefield

Mohanty, Talpade Chandra. 2006. *Feminism without borders.* Durham, NC: Duke University Press.

Nurowska, Maria. 1992. *Panny i wdowy.* PKN: Warsaw.

Obrebka, Elzbieta. 1994. Businesswoman. *Sukces* 11: 5.

Penn, Shana. 2005. *Solidarity's secret.* Ann Arbor, MI: University of Michigan Press.

Petersen, T., and L.A. Morgan. 2001. The within-job gender wage gap. In D. Grusky (ed.), *Social stratification: Class, race, and gender in sociological perspective.* Boulder, CO: Westview Press.

Polska jest Kobieta. 2007. Organization Polish Women. Retrieved on May 2, 2007, at http://www.polskajestkobieta.org/index.php.

Rueschmeyer, Marilyn. 1998. *Women in the politics of postcommunist Eastern Europe.* New York: Sharpe.

Rzeczpospolita. 1995. *Appendix: Work-Specialists* 21, January 25.

Schaeffer, R.K. 2003. *Understanding globalization: The social consequences of political, economic, and environmental change.* Lanham, MD: Rowman & Littlefield.

Seguino, S. 1997. Export-led growth and persistence of gender inequality in the newly industrialized countries. In J.M. Rives and M. Yousefi (eds.), *Economic dimensions of gender inequality: A global perspective.* Westport, CT: Praeger.

Standing, G. 1989. Global feminization through flexible labor. *World Development* 17: 1077–1095

Twoj Styl. 2005. *Opowiem ci o Sierpniu* 8: 14.

Urban, Jerzy. 1972. Kitchen or life. *Polityka:* 44, October 26.

U.S. Bureau of the Census. 1993. Money income of households, families, and persons in the United States: 1992. *Current Population Reports Consumer Income Series*, pp. 60–184. U.S. Department of Commerce. Washington, DC: U.S. Government Printing Office.

Vagneron, Isabell. 2000. From urban areas to rice fields: Subcontractors and home workers in the Thai garment sector. CERDI–CNRS, Université d'Auvergne, Clermont-Ferrand. Working papers. Retrieved on May 20, 2009, at www.agents.cirad.fr/index.php/Isabelle+VAGNERON/Publications.

Wałęsa, Leszek. 1990. *Droga nadziei.* PKW: Warsaw.

Wejnert, Barbara. 2003. The effects of growth of democracy and transition to market-based economies on women's well-being. *Journal of Consumer Policy* 26: 465–493.

_____. 2005. Diffusion, development and democracy, 1800–1999. *American Sociological Review* 70: 53–81.

Wejnert, Barbara, and Almagul Djumabaeva. 2003. From patriarchy to egalitarism? Parental roles in democratizing Poland and Kyrgyzstan. *Marriage and Family Review* 3-4: 147–173.

Wroblewski, A.K. 1972. Someone must be at the bottom. An interview with Prof. Ewa

Kagan-Kans, Vice-Rector for Women at Indiana University. *Polityka* 45, November 4.

Yu, W. 2001. Family demands, gender attitudes, and married women's labor force participation: Comparing Japan and Taiwan. In M.C. Brinton (ed.), *Women's working lives in East Asia.* Standford, CA: Standford University Press.

_____. 2001. Taking informality into account: Women's work in the formal and informal sectors in Taiwan. In M.C. Brinton (ed.), *Women's working lives in East Asia.* Standford, CA: Standford University Press.

Name_____

Test Your Knowledge: Chapter 5

Short Answer Questions

1. In contemporary societies persist attitude that women have about them-selves that they are unable to perform the task as well as men **do**. Tradi-tional believes, such as, women should not educate themselves if they want to have family because after completed higher education they will be too old to have children or to find husband, adds to the downgraded self-perception of women. Explain, the impact of such attitudes on employers' evaluation of women's work using the concept of wage gap.

2. Define "feminization of labor" using the theory of globalization. Provide at least three studies or empirical investigations explaining the process.

3. Define four factor indicated by Peterson and Morgan as causes of gender inequality at work.

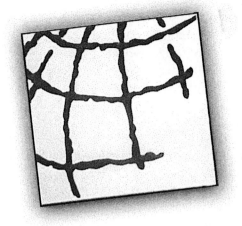

6

Challenges to Women Empowerment through Science and Technology Interventions

Although developed and developing countries proclaim promotion of gender equality and undertake measures to empower women, unequal representation of women in science, the industrial labor force, and technology exists across countries globally. Observed outcomes of empowerment initiatives reveal a limited scope of undertaken initiatives that could generate women empowerment.

One such initiative is the eradication of the unequal representation of women in science, the industrial labor force, and technology that exists across countries globally. Female talent and resources are under-utilized despite their great potential to contribute toward the social and economic development. Comprising more than half of the global population, women could play an immeasurable role in global development. Therefore, various major international initiatives have been undertaken on the subject.

One such initiative was the United Nations' Decades on Women and Development (1975–1995). With resolution 3520, the United Nations proclaimed the period from 1976 to 1985 to be the United Nations' Decade for Women: Equality, Development, and Peace, on December 15, 1975 (United Nations 1976). Special attention was directed toward the role of women in global development, including their participation and empowerment through science and technology. Gender equality is also one of the eight United Nations' Millennium Development Goals, which calls for action to empower women, including empowerment related to science and technology.

More than three decades after the United Nations' proclamation of Decades on Women and Development, the initiation of policies to promote equal participation of women in relation to men in technical and scientific professions remains to be one of the essential paths in achieving gender parity and women empowerment despite a country's level of development and its placement within the global economy.

Contrary to popular belief, throughout the modern era of technological and scientific discoveries, increasing societal education level, and paid labor force participation of women, women have experienced far more discrimination with regard to their employment status, earning abilities, and achievement in science and technology. The unequal position of women in terms of their involvement in technological and scientific professions is observed in developed and developing countries, and across states with democratic and non-democratic political system. As Michael Binyon (1983, 36) so cogently noted, it is "true that in Russia women keep the wheels of industry turning. Virtually no factory could keep going without the female labor, no hospitals could function in a country where women constitute about 70 percent of all doctors, and service industry would collapse without women hairdressers and waitresses, ticket-sellers, and shop assistants . . . "

At the same time, despite the prioritization of gender equality, the earning capacities of women lag behind that of men (Binyon 1983). Moreover, access of women to technologically based work is limited. Therefore, the presence of women in blue-collar jobs and engineering, mathematics, and finance jobs in well-developed and developing countries is persistently stereotyped as a representation of women in "nontraditional jobs," and classified as women involvement in "typical male fields."

Women in Science and Technology in the Well-Developed United States

Employment. Since 1950, despite the continued increase of women participation in the labor force in the United States across all age categories (see Figure 6.1), women are continuously combating the invisible barriers that are strong enough to hold women back from top-level jobs simply because they are women rather than because they lack job-relevant skills, education, or experience. Such a barrier is called the glass ceiling, and it depicts an exclusion of women from top management positions.

The glass ceiling has prevented women from getting ahead in the work force. Although women's participation in the U.S. labor force has increased, and women occupy 44 percent of management jobs in American companies, top management ranks remain dominated by men. Consequently, by 2008 only 3 to 5 percent of the top management jobs in private sector companies are filled by women.

Managerial Positions. One of the most powerful ways to shatter the glass ceiling is to increase women presence at the top managerial positions (see Figure 6.2).

The higher the percentage of lower-level management jobs filled by women, the more likely the establishment will have women in top

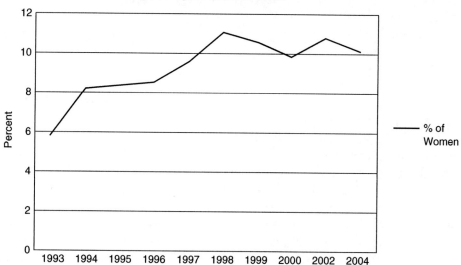

Figure 6.1

Source: Figure compiled using data from Statistical Abstract of the United States, U.S. Census Bureau, versions 1995–2008; data from the Society of Women Engineers (2009); and data from National Science Foundation and the United States, U.S. Census Bureau.

management positions. Research shows that the greater the emphasis on promotion and development, the more likely the establishment will have women in top management positions. Nonetheless, as of today, more women hold blue-collar jobs than managerial positions. *Blue-collar* refers to jobs performed by those who work for wages, especially manual or industrial laborers. Examples include construction jobs, ironworkers, electricians, carpenters, stone masons, and surveyors.

Being a substantial minority, women formed organizations to provide support to their issues and rights. Among the organizations that support women in blue-collar jobs are Tradeswomen, Inc., which provides fair and safe conditions for women who work in the building

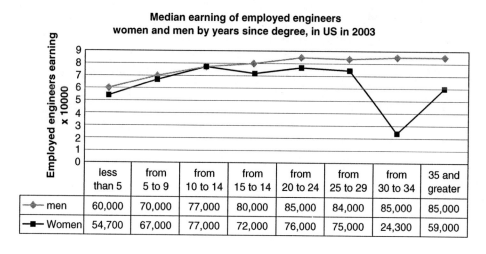

	less than 5	from 5 to 9	from 10 to 14	from 15 to 14	from 20 to 24	from 25 to 29	from 30 to 34	35 and greater
men	60,000	70,000	77,000	80,000	85,000	84,000	85,000	85,000
Women	54,700	67,000	77,000	72,000	76,000	75,000	24,300	59,000

Figure 6.2

Source: Figure compiled using data from Statistical Abstract of the United States, U.S. Census Bureau, versions 1995–2008; National Science Foundation 2000; and National Science Board 2000.

trades, and the Office for Women's Rights at the City of Seattle, which develops special recruitment programs and workshops to provide information to women.

Blue-collar work is not the only area in which women are underrepresented. Similar situation exists among women in engineering. For the last three decades, the number of women engineers has been steadily increasing, but only about one out of ten engineers is a woman. To stimulate women to achieve full potential in careers as engineers and leaders, and to expend the image of the engineering profession as a positive force in improving the quality of life and to demonstrate the value of diversity, women engineers formed the Society for Women Engineers. Across the broad spectrum of the U.S. engineering jobs, salaries for women engineers remain much smaller than for male engineers (see Figure 6.3).

Women are visibly underrepresented at the top position not only in science and technology, but also in finance. These positions, commonly thought of as jobs on Wall Street (the financial center of the United States in New York), are characterized by salaries at the top income brackets in the country. Women, being a minority on Wall Street, face frequent gender discrimination in promotion to the highest positions and in increase of salaries in comparison to men. Some known discrimination cases brought by women to courts against their companies include Salomon Smith Barney, Goldman Sachs, Morgan Stanley, and Merrill Lynch. In a few cases, after winning the discrimination cases, women were able to break through the glass ceiling and land in the executive suites of these companies. The Equal Employment Opportunity Commission (EEOC) has been designing rules to ensure women are well represented at the top levels of financial firms.

Despite an increasing representation of women on Wall Street, women are still vastly underrepresented in the top ranks and climbing in the ranks of managing directors relatively slowly—17 percent in 2003 compared with 13 percent in 2001 (National Science Foundation 2000). In addition, the economic downturn negatively affects the overall percentage of women working on Wall Street (such employment declined to 37 percent in 2003 from 41 percent in 2001 and 43 percent in 1999).

Women's Movement. To organize themselves and to have their voices heard, women in finance organized the annual Women on Wall Street Conference, a meeting addressing issues faced by women on Wall Street. These conferences were initially attended by only 350 people, but participation grew to 2,000 men and women by 2003. Some positive outcomes came out of such meetings. For example, after the meeting in 2003, the Deutsche Bank offered mentoring circles and an additional 12 weeks' paid leave after maternity leave.

Women in Science and Technology in Developing Countries

Women representation in science and technology is severely challenged in developing countries. For example, in developing Eastern European countries, the number of working women steadily increased over the decades following World War II, however, the concentration of female

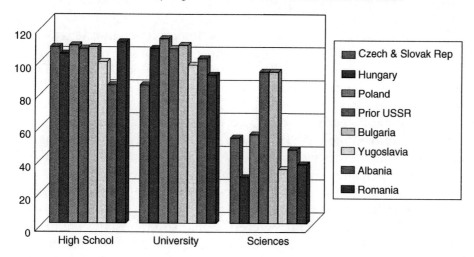

Figure 6.3

Source: Figure was created using data from "Human Developement Report 1992" p. 191. All figures are expressed in relation to the male average, which is indexes to equal 100. The smaller the figure the bigger the gap, the closer the figure to 100 the smaller the gap and a figure above 100 indicates that the female average is higher than the male.

workforce was in agriculture, unskilled industrial, and low-skilled service sector jobs, such as secretarial, accounting, and sales (Drakulic 1993, Titkov 1984). These jobs typically were ranked as not difficult and, consequently, resulted in lower wages. In Czechoslovakia and Yugoslavia, the average wage for women was only 68 percent and 60 to 80 percent, respectively, of the average wage of men (Drakulic 1993). In Hungary, where the earning opportunities for women has improved since the 1980s but has reached only the level of 70 percent of men's wages, the fundamental gender-based division of labor was never eradicated (Lampland 1990).

With the transition toward global economy, the situation in the labor market worsened, affecting the opportunities for women employment and achievement, especially in typically science and engineering professions (Amott and Matthaei 1996).

Employment. In the early years of transition, rising unemployment has been a particular threat to citizens' sense of security, but women have suffered most from the declines in employment (Wejnert and Spencer 1996). Institution of democracy and associated with that market economy in post-communist countries led to decrease of the need for laborers, and women were first laid off from jobs or were able to hold on the very low paid and least prestige jobs (Wejnert 1996). Such trends caused, on one hand, the rapid increase of women among the registered unemployed and, on the other, an increase of the gender gap in earning between female and male workers. Although more women than men were registered as unemployed, women received lower unemployment benefits than men in all East European and Russian countries because of the gender gap in earning in Communist time and because unemployment benefits were structured according to wage rates. For example, in Hungary in 1991, 79 percent of unemployed women (as compared to 55 percent of unemployed men) received benefits lower than the official minimum wage. At the same time, one-seventh of all families were headed by a single female, accounting for the rearing of almost one-sixth of the children below 15 years of age (Wejnert 1996).

Similarly, in Poland in the 1991, the unemployment rate was 13 percent (in 1999, about 10 percent), and three times more women than men registered as unemployed although the number of jobs offered to men was seven times higher than to women. By the end of October 1990, women constituted 51 percent of the 1 million unemployed, and 37.3 percent unemployed women for every vacancy compared with 9.5 percent unemployed men. By 1994, men constituted 58.8 percent of the overall labor, whereas women constituted 44 percent. But out of the overall 13.9 percent unemployed, women constituted more than half (52.2 percent), whereas men 47.8 percent of the total number (Polish Statistical Office 1995).

Women in other countries faced similar situations. In Bulgaria, in the mid-1990s, 43.1 percent of employed women expressed fear that they would lose their jobs, as compared with 38.5 percent of employed men (Petrova 1993). Access to the better-paying, professional jobs, such as in engineering, law, top business administration, and managerial, was at best limited for women. In Bulgaria, only 1.6 percent of women worked in management, decision-making, and higher administrative spheres in 1988. In Yugoslavia, although the number of working women steadily increased from 26 percent in 1961 to 36 percent in 1981, the number of women in managerial positions steadily decreased from 15 percent in 1962 to 12 percent 1981 (Ojulic 1995). Contrary to popular belief, during the period of democratic transition and consolidation of democracy greater gender asymmetry was created, particularly in the professional field of science and technology. Lower earnings and lower positions were in sharp contrast to the significant strides that had been made by women in educational attainment at the university level.

Education. In former Soviet Bloc states, the number of female university students grew from 23 percent of the total number of students in 1948–1949 to more than 50 percent in 1988–1989, reaching a ratio of 24 percent of female students to the total number of women aged 20 to 24 years old. In comparison, the ratio for men was 23 percent (United Nations Development Program 1992).

By the beginning of the transition to democracy in 1989–1990, women represented 56 percent of all specialists with a secondary education or with two years of collegiate education, and 38 percent of specialists with at least full university degrees (Siklova 1993). At the start of the 1990s, when the number of school-aged girls was equal to the number of school-aged boys, female students in secondary schools (high schools) outnumbered male students in Poland, Hungary, Czechoslovakia, and the Soviet Union. At the same time, female students composed more than half of the university student population in almost all former Soviet Bloc countries (e.g., in Poland 52 percent, in Hungary 53 percent) (Polish Statistical Office 1993, 430; Hungarian Statistical Office 1993, 67–71; United Nations Development Program 1992, 191).

In the Soviet Union, there was an equal percentage of female and male students majoring in the previously predominantly "male" specialties of science at universities (see Figure 6.4). Thus, it is clear that the differential wages and occupational positions between men and women were not due to an inferior educational background for women.

Managerial and Administrative Positions. Gender asymmetry was broaden due to the limited representation of women on the managerial or public domain positions (Olujic 1995). For example, in 1982 in East Germany, women constituted 33.6 percent of the People Chamber (parliament) but no women held positions in the Politburo (a governing body), and only one women served as a minister (in the ministry of education). In 1983 in Hungary, women held only 27 percent of the National Assembly members and only 3 out of 21 minister positions. In the transitional democracy of Poland, women represented only 10.45 percent of members in *Sejm* (Polish parliament) and 1 percent in *Senate* of the post-communist parliament in 1994 (Polish Statistical Office 1995). There was only one woman minister and only one woman as committee chair in the Polish government. Although deputy positions held by women in Poland increased from 12.4 percent in 1964 to 23 percent in 1983, they still constituted the lowest female representation among the Eastern European countries. Similarly, only 10 out of 102 judges in the Polish Supreme Court were women.

Although women's under-representation in governing bodies could be a result of women's reduced interest in politics, an analysis of women political dissidents of the 1970s and 1980s does not support such a hypothesis. Over the period of political struggle for democracy in East Central Europe, women were represented equally to men in democratic, oppositional movements.

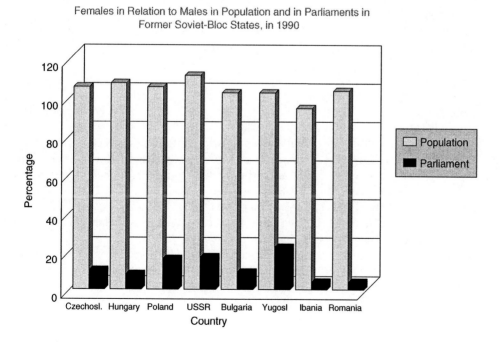

Figure 6.4

Source: All figures are expressed in relation to the male average, which is indexes to equal 100. The smaller the figure the bigger gap, the closer the figure to 100 the smaller the gap and a figure above 100 indicates that the female average is higher than male. *Source:* United Nations, 1992. Human Develpment Report, p. 191.

In contrast to their broad participation in the network of political opposition, but following the pattern of women under representation in governments, leaders of dissident movements excluded women from major political activity (Wejnert 2002).

Summary and Concluding Remarks

The gender gap in academic science is a topic of ongoing policy and scholarly debates. Studies in fields as diverse as engineering and biology have found that women scientists suffer from an attainment gap along at least three important dimensions: productivity, recognition, and reward (Waverly, Murray, and Stuart 2006, 665). The limited evidence that exists about "academic entrepreneurship," such as patenting, consulting, and scientific advisory boards, also suggests a gender gap of considerable magnitude

The comparison of women participating in science and technology in the democratic United States and newly democratizing countries adds to this debate. As a presented study indicates, an introduction of civil freedom, equal rights, and democratic principles is not a sufficient measure of the possibilities and opportunities that are open to women. The case studies showed gender disparity in the representation of women in science and technology. The establishment of policies promoting gender equality in high-prestige and well-paid positions becomes only the initial step on the path of opening access to professional fields that are relatively close to women. Stereotypical perceptions of women's low potential to achieve in science seem to constitute additional constrains. Such a hypothesis would need to be tested in the future. However, if the testing would turn out to be positive, it would shed light on the problem of interdependency of democratization and limited women representation in engineering and science, limited earning capacities, and the gender gap in participating in scientific entrepreneurship.

References

Amott, Teresa, and Julie Matthaei. 1996. *Race, gender and work.* Boston: South End Press.

Binyon, Michael. 1983. *Life in Russia.* New York: Pantheon Books.

Drakulic, Slavenka. 1993. Women and new democracy in the former Yugoslavia. In Nanette Funk and Magda Mueller (eds.), *Gender politics and post-communism.* New York: Routledge.

Hungarian Statistical Office. 1993. *Mayar Statisztikai Zsebkonyv,* pp. 67–71.

Lampland, Martha. 1989. Unthinkable subjects: Women and labor in socialist Hungary. *East European Quarterly* 4: 389–398.

National Science Board. 2000. *Toward a more effective NSF role in international science and engineering. Report.* Retrieved on March 13, 2009 at www.nsf.gov/nsb/documents/2000/nsb00217/nsb00217.htm

National Science Foundation. 2000. *Science and engineering indicators.* Arlington, VA: National Science Board.

Olujic, Maria. 1995. Economic and demographic change in contemporary Yugoslavia: Persistence of traditional gender ideology. *East European Quarterly* 4: 477–485.

Petrova, Dimitrina. 1993. The winding road to emancipation in Bulgaria. In Nanette Funk and Magda Mueller (eds.), *Gender politics and post-communism,* New York: Routledge.

Polish Statistical Office. 1993. *Rocznik Statystyczny*, p. 80.

Polish Statistical Office, 1995. *Rocznik Statystyczny*, p. 81.

Siklova, Jirina. 1993. Are women in Central and Eastern Europe conservative? In Nanette Funk and Magda Mueller (eds.), *Gender politics and post-communism*, New York: Routledge.

Titkov, Anna. 1993. Political change in Poland: Cause, modifier, or barrier to gender equality. In Nanette Funk and Magda Mueller (eds.), *Gender politics and post-communism*. New York: Routledge.

United Nations Development Program. 1992. *Human development report*. New York: Oxford University Press.

United Nations. 1976. United Nations conference on science and technology for development. Retrieved on January 2009 at www.un-documents.net/a31r184.htm

Waverly, Ding, Fiona Murray, and Toby Stuart. 2006. Gender differences in patenting in the academic life sciences. *Science* 313: 665–667.

Wejnert, Barbara. 1996. Political transition and gender transformation in the communist and post-communist periods. In Barbara Wejnert and Metta Spencer (eds.), *Women in post-communism*. Greenwich, CT: JAI Press.

_____. 2002. The contribution of collective protests to the softening of communist regimes in East Central Europe. In Barbara Wejnert (ed.), *Transition to democracy in Eastern Europe and Russia*. Westport, CT: Greenwood Press.

Wejnert, Barbara, and Metta Spencer. 1996. *Women in post-communism*. Greenwich, CT: JAI Press.

Name_____

Test Your Knowledge: Chapter 6

Essay Questions

1. Define and justify the meaning of the statement "When mothers health suffer, all nations do as well."

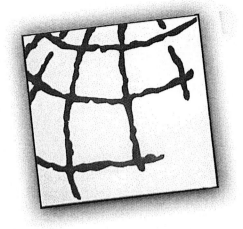

Global Development and Women's Health

7

Global issues are present in all areas of life. They affect countries' economies, political situations, culture, policies, and citizens' well-being. The multitude and complexities of their impact can be seen in everyday existence. The issue of **women's health** in the globalized world, however, germinates as substantially more essential, as influenced by broad areas of societal existence and societal future development. It becomes interconnected—although it may not seem so at first—with all aspects of human life, with individuals abilities and capacity to develop physically, psychologically, and intellectually. It affects the capability of critical thinking and the processes for making decisions concerning the progress of human civilization. Women's health is often forgotten and seems to be irrelevant in comparison to macro-structural, global concerns. However, because the health of mothers strengthens the foundation of all nations and, consequently, of the world's future, maternal health reflects the survival and future prosperity of local communities, nations, and the global milieu.

Conceptualization of Women's Health Issues

The Millennium Development Goals Initiative of the United Nations (United Nations 2008) provide a shared vision of a much-improved world by 2015, in which extreme poverty is cut in half, child and maternal mortality is greatly reduced, gender disparities in primary and secondary education are eliminated, women are more empowered, and health and environment indicators are improved. With this eight-point agenda, the last few years have seen a change in the concept of global development, which now encompasses health, social, political, technological, economic, and human growth—and not merely economic growth. In the midst of all the spectacular progress on the global development goals forum, we are still faced with many concerns that need to be addressed. Yet only minimal efforts have been made to directly integrate health concerns as a priority into development processes.

The interface between health, technology, and wider society can play a pivotal role in enhancing the quality of life of people. The relationship between health and development has undergone renewed scrutiny. There is a search for new models to deal with global threats, soaring medical costs, technological costs, gender disparity, poverty, and disease. Technological innovation offers a unique opportunity for partnership between health and global development to change the pattern of work and enhance health-promoting habits.

A study conducted by the World Bank, titled "Development in Practice, Improving Women's Health in India," has pointed out that investing in women's health is now being recognized as an essential component of social and economic growth. Investments in women's health can be argued on several grounds, such as equity and human rights and existing gender disparity, multiple benefits of women's improved health, such as the impact of the mother's health on her offspring and cost-effectiveness of reproductive health interventions. It is essential to view the health of women in a holistic way within the social, economic, and political context of their lives. The health of a country's female population ensures health and education of the next generation and economic well-being of households.

Many problems of women's health are still not addressed properly at this point. For example, research and experience from several countries have shown that a majority of maternal deaths occur in the post-partum period and more than half within a day of delivery (Steinmetz 2008). Having a medical professional or a skilled medical attendant at every birth is the single critical factor that could save many lives of mothers. But that is easier said than done. For example, in India, the second National Family Health survey conducted in 1998 and 1999 found that only 14.8 percent of pregnant women delivered at a health facility, whereas the rest did so at home.

It has been argued that maternal deaths could be reduced by addressing women health factors alone. Emergency care services (including transport, regular visits and record-keeping by nurses or trained attendants), safe abortion services, and post-natal care for women can make a huge difference. A great proportion of girls conceive for the first time during their teenage years (before age of 18). For example, half the girls in Rajasthan (India) conceive on an average at 17.6 years (Wejnert, Steimentz, and Prakash 2008). Almost half of Nepalese women are married and have children before they are 18 years old and, in Hindu communities, early marriages before menstruation (at age 13 or 14) are the most preferred. A girl conceiving before her eighteenth birthday has a 2.5 percent higher chance of dying than one who is more than 18 years old. Most girls are undernourished, anemic, and cannot sustain healthy pregnancies (Prakash 2009). Other issues of concern during global development include women literacy levels, family size, preference for sons, unsafe abortions, deliveries by untrained personnel and lack of proper emergency obstetrics care.

The health status of women in the world is impacted by social, cultural, and economic variables. Most women still lack decision-making power at the family and community level and do not have control over resources. Thus, they lack control over their reproductive rights, leading to a high maternal mortality rate.

TABLE 3.1	A List of Maternal Health Issues by Thematic Area	
THEMATIC AREA	**WOMENT HEALTH ISSUE**
Concept of Women's Health in Relation to Globalization	Influences on women's health: diffusing democracy and market economy; global communication system; local vs. global culture including Western biases; global development; technological innovations
Exemplification of Women's Health Problems	Cross-world unsecured women's health issues in globalizing, transitional societies; low developed countries; post-industrial, modern countries
Research and Practice	Medical professionals and practitioners remediation

Sources: Table was comprised based on literary material on women's health issues, (Annan 2004; Koop, Pearson and Schwarz 2002).

There is an urgent need to understand various issues concerning women's health and, consequently, to alert policy, institutional, and peoples' initiatives at various levels worldwide to ensure sustainable, equitable, and just development for women and their families. This situation needs the attention of academicians, medical professionals, women's studies centers, social scientists, non-governmental organizations (NGOs), administrators, policy makers, national governments, United Nations, and international agencies.

It is in this context that the topic of women's health is highly relevant and apt. The challenge is in understanding processes and principles involved in safe motherhood and finding the best practices and innovative strategies that have been successful in improving maternal health and in reducing maternal mortality.

The emerging women's health concerns can be organized within a conceptual framework that links together approaches to research on women's reproductive health, processes involved in maternal care, relevant policies, societal infrastructures, and the effects of global economic and political processes on women's health. The framework is supported by case studies on specific medical problems, strategies, and policies concerning women.

Women health issues can be grouped into three thematic areas, shown in Table 3.1. There are also other possible categorizations and approaches to global women health that are not covered in this chapter. This chapter covers the most important concerns in each of the categories in Table 3.1 that are less frequently addressed or that need an urgent attention.

Main Concerns of Global Women's Health

Generally, the most fruitful understanding of women's health issues is to view these problems as an affordable health for women and their families based on an application of appropriate measures and technology. The holistic approach to the worldwide health of women is connected to processes of diffusing globalization. It provides an answer on why global development is costly to women health (Wejnert 2003). The implementation of gender equality exemplified by women's health could reverse the trends reported by the United Nations Commission on the Status of Women, which found that women produce more than 50 percent of food worldwide (in African countries more than 90 percent), but women constitute the majority of the 22 million people who die yearly from starvation, malnutrition, and lack of medical care (Morgan 1984).

Scholars frequently address issues of using modern communication strategies to promote adequate and appropriate information regarding women's health. Accurate strategic messaging at the national and global level could enable planners and policy makers to take appropriate courses of action related to population health and sustainable development. At the most basic level, more adequate and appropriate information concerning women's health is conducive to informed, responsible decision-making concerning sexual and reproductive behavior, family planning and family life, and a protected, healthy, and safe life of mothers and children (Vijaykumar 2008).

Often ignorance and lack of scientific information result in policies (both formal and informal) that negatively women's health. In other cases, cultural or social norms drive policy decisions. Depending on the development of their infrastructure, scientific understanding, reliance on myths to understand their environment, and social norms, culture attributes different motivations, benefits, and approaches to issues of women and maternal health. For example, most health care professionals agree that breastfeeding is preferable for infants and babies, but there is widespread disagreement about how long a baby should be nursed or if a baby should be nursed if mother has serious health problems (e.g., HIV) (Parrott and Cumming 2008). Preventing ill-informed decisions that impact negatively on the lives of people throughout the globe is critical not only in developing health policies that are appropriate and effective, but also critical in focusing on the correct information about human physiology and human health behaviors.

The problem of understanding of women's health in the context of the main concerns of global development could be addressed as the process of interconnected private-public partnership in reference to women health. The concept of public and private partnership is increasingly promoted as a panacea to build and capitalize on the existing personnel and monetary and material/non-material resources inherent in social organizations and communities. Drawing from empirical research conducted in African Senegal and Mali (Lo 2008) and globalizing, post-communist Ukraine (Romaniuk 2002), a critical examination of the challenges and opportunities reveals issues deterrent to improving women's health in merging to globally developed countries. For example, many developing countries are faced with withdrawal or limitation of state funds supporting health initiatives. Others problems are the decentralization of health policies, increasing retrenchment from the state, and scarcity of financial and human resources in the health sector. Innovative approaches and sustainable solutions to the pervasive deficit of resources in health—and especially women's health—is one of the key issues faced by gender within global development.

This theme is further developed within a discourse on medical innovations and medical research findings that facilitate a better understanding of women's reproductive health but are not always recognized or acknowledged by policy makers as emerging issues in the thematic area of women's global health. Research referring to the antenatal care, psychological indicators of women health gains an understanding of the illness pattern, through experiential learning and problem-solving. Examples from clinical psychological work in India show the detrimental impact of post-partum disorders on the well-being of infants and mothers (Daniel 2009).

Determinants of Women's Health

The status of women is often one measure of the level of societal development. Status is based on the cultural beliefs and traditions regarding the patriarchy and the laws that are used to control women—and sanctions when women disregard these laws. This status can be measured directly by factors such as the level of education, age of marriage, inheritance laws, and life expectancy. Gender-based inequalities that exist in patriarchal societies result in males playing a critical role in determining the education and employment of family members, age at marriage, access to and utilization of health, nutrition, and social services for women and children.

Culture and tradition. Regardless of their personal beliefs, women in countries dominated by the strongly traditional religions may have their health care options limited and/or be under the control of a hierarchy of males. In many countries that follow orthodox Muslim beliefs, a woman must be covered not only to protect her modesty, but more importantly to protect the property belonging to the males in her family (i.e., the woman herself). In other cultures, women are also forced to live in physical seclusion (*Purdah*), which is practiced by Muslims and various Hindus. The conditions of body covering and seclusion severely limit women's freedom of movement, including visiting health care facilities. Beliefs regarding ritual pollution and ritual segregation during child birth and afterwards result in compromised health care and nutrition (Bhattarai 2008).

It is important to recognize that women's autonomy, independences, and access to resources may not necessarily be linked to wealth. Their isolation and limited freedom of movement results in their being totally dependent on males (fathers, father-in-law, husbands, and adult sons when widowed) and restricts access to family planning, health information, and services (Conly and Camp 1992, Coale and Banister 1996). For example, in Saudi Arabia, even wealthy, well-educated women are not permitted to drive a car.

There are also indirect indicators of the value of women, such as sex-selective abortion (female feticide) in China after the one-child policy was enacted. Female feticide and female infanticide are common occurrences in countries where sons provide a safety-net for their parents in old age and daughters cost money at the time of marriage but do not contribute to parent security in old age. (Daughters become integrated parts of their husband's family.) Poor families in certain parts of the world resort to killing second and subsequent births of daughters to avoid an unwanted burden on family resources at time of their marriage.

Education. Low level of literacy and limited education are problems faced by many societies that experience resource-insufficiency. Women who may not be able to access information or assistance even when available are particularly affected. If they are not literate, their world is limited to only those people with whom they have personal contact. These women will unlikely be well informed about safe practices for pregnancy, delivery, and post-partum care, or any other concerns typical for women's health. Information about available resources that is passed from person to person may not only be inaccurate but also dangerous.

Political and economic characteristics. Finally, the political and economic structure of each society also determines opportunities regarding women's health. The expansion of economic growth under a capitalist market economy results in greatly improved conditions for all citizens when the economy stabilizes. Thus, basic health care security is greatly improved when economic prosperity takes places, but it is impoverished during economic difficulties observed at time of transition to global market economy. Cross-country analysis of the effects of emerging capitalism on women's health and women's life span found that health care in general has deteriorated (Wejnert 2003).

Practical Suggestions and Remediation Policy Implications

Research finds that factors that influence women's health care include culture and tradition, governmental policies or the lack of such policies, education, technology, and available resources. Therefore, practical suggestions and remediation offered by researchers, medical professionals, and practitioners suggest that to improve women's health, national and international networking should directly focus on interventions. It is recognized that as far as safe women's health is concerned, women live dangerously through their life. Safe and adequate women's health could be achieved if there is a shift in perception with adequate understanding of the socio-cultural and economic status of woman, which includes the work burden of women (Lewin et al. 2001).

Currently, 260 million people live below the poverty line, one of every two children under three years of age is malnourished, nearly 1.8 million infants die each year, every 4 minutes a woman dies in childbirth or due to pregnancy-related causes, and discrimination against girl children continues. For every woman who loses her life, there are approximately 20 additional women who will suffer injury, infection, and both short- or long-term disabilities resulting from inadequate prenatal, delivery, and post-natal care (World Health Organization 2006). The challenge is to bridge these widening disparities. The immediate need is to translate policies into measures that would improve social services and empower women and children throughout the world. Having goals in mind, cross-national research demonstrates that safe women's health initiatives need to be addressed holistically. This means taking into account mothers' physical, mental, and social conditions in the treatment of women illnesses and establishing pro-safe women's health policies.

The holistic approach should include the understanding of women's needs of health care and social concerns. Consequently such approach should include issues of:

- Gender equality in societies
- Less domestic violence
- Increased school enrollment
- Increased entrepreneurship
- Job security for women
- Better access to health care
- Increased civil participation
- Better infrastructure of transportation and communication

The overall focus on the processes and outcomes of the worldwide globalization to women's health are being expressed by interdisciplinary scholars and health practitioners from Eastern Europe, America, Asia, and Africa, as well as prominent policy figures, including members of international organization (e.g., UNICEF), government members, and directors of non-governmental organizations. The need of special attention paid to pro-women's health policies and services can be best summarized by a statement of Kofi Annan, Secretary General of the United Nations, who said, "Study after study has shown that there is no effective development strategy in which women do not play a central role. When women are fully involved, the benefits can be seen immediately: families are healthier; they are better fed; their income, savings and reinvestment go up. And what is true of families is true of communities and, eventually, of whole countries" (Annan 2004).

Sharing Lessons on HIV/AIDS Prevention: Techniques for Youth in Rural Areas (Preliminary Report)

by Eunice Rodriguez, Stanford University and Josephine Allen, Cornell University

INTRODUCTION

The turn of the century coincided with an increase in the incidence of HIV in many rural areas in North America (Berry 2000) and, according to the Office of National AIDS Policy, 25 percent of the new HIV infections in the United States are estimated to occur among people under the age of 20.

The CDC reports that between 1,039,000 and 1,185,000 persons in the United States were living with HIV/AIDS by the end of 2003, and about a quarter of those were unaware of their HIV infection (Glynn and Rhodes 2005). It is estimated that between 40,000 and 80,000 Americans become infected with HIV each year. According to the Office of National AIDS Policy: "Under current trends, that means that between 27 and 54 young people in the United States under the age of 20 are infected by HIV each day, or more than two young people every hour" (National AIDS Policy 1996). In addition, the United States has one the highest rates of sexually transmitted diseases in the developed world (Singh and Darroch 1996).

Continued

There is a growing consensus that education on HIV/AIDS prevention should begin at an early age and be reinforced beyond the classroom. It is also beginning to be realized that adolescents must become a more important part of the research process (National AIDS Policy 1996).

Responses to the problem of rising HIV incidence in rural areas must be sensitive to local conditions. In contrast with urban areas, where population concentrations can sustain interventions tailored to groups of people with specific and/or shared constellations of risk, rural populations are dispersed, risks are diverse and variable, existing educational interventions are often general and euphemistic, and the dynamics of risk behaviors are relatively uncharted. There is little published research about interventions that have been demonstrated to reduce HIV-related risks among rural adolescents in the United States.

This situation prompted the implementation of an HIV prevention intervention, tailored to the unique needs of rural residents. The preliminary report of the pilot study conducted with Josephine Allen, Ph.D., and Jennifer Tiffany, Ph.D., discusses the use of a participant-driven recruitment (PDR) approach (Bianchi et al. 2003, Heckathorn et al. 1998, Kusi-Appouh 2006, Salganik and Heckathorn 2004, Tiffany 2006) as part of an HIV/AIDS youth prevention intervention in Cortland County, New York.

EVALUATION AND DISCUSSION

In the study, PDR/RDS (PDR/RDS: respondent driven sample) techniques were successful in identifying a sample of participants (a total of 128), mirroring the composition of the population in the target county in terms of gender, race/ethnicity, and location (town/outside of the town). Participation rates by young men (50 percent of the sample), residents of small villages/farming communities (23 percent), and youth of color (13 percent) were higher than those obtained in previous studies.

We found that those with moderate or low knowledge scores were about three times less likely to recruit highly knowledgeable people, even after controlling for demographic characteristics such as gender, ethnicity, age, location, and living arrangements. Other specific behaviors, such as having had sex or using condoms during intercourse, were not predictive of recruiting people with similar experiences.

Of a total of 128 participants who completed baseline surveys (including questions on knowledge, worry, and risk behavior) and participated in the educational sessions and PDR effort, we were able to locate 72 of the participants to collect follow-up information in 2003. Comparison of follow-up to baseline data indicated an increase in HIV/AIDS knowledge and understanding. There was a 10 percent increase in the average number of correct answers among questions regarding abstinence, condom use, and sexual transmission of the disease. We also observed a decrease of HIV/AIDS-related worries, which is consistent with previous literature that indicates that as the knowledge levels increase, worry levels decrease (Krauss, Tiffany, and Goldsamt 1997).

The lack of a comparison group precludes a rigorous assessment of the possible impact of this intervention. However, to illustrate how the sexual behavior of the program participants at follow-up compared to other U.S. youth, we presented data from the National Youth Risk Behavior Survey (NYRBS). Abstention rates of 16- and 17-year-old participants in the Cortland project were higher than both the national and the rural areas average, but no difference was appreciated among 18 year olds. However, the percentage of 18-year-old project participants reporting condom use was greater than for 18-year-old NYRBS respondents.

NEXT STEPS AND LESSONS LEARNED

Recruitment network analysis suggests that patterns of affiliation by gender and residency can inform the development of culturally sensitive educational interventions. Our project also confirms that the PDR/RDS techniques are successful in stimulating the participation of adolescents in risk prevention programs in nonmetropolitan areas. Evaluation comments of adolescent participants and facilitators illustrated the benefits of the PDR/RDS method (Bianchi et al. 2003).

Our project can be replicated elsewhere. Both the recruitment method and the peer-led educational exercises based on the "Talking with Kids about HIV/AIDS" curriculum can be used for developing risk reduction activities for teenagers.

More attention to the behaviors, attitudes, knowledge, and worries of rural teens is warranted in the assessment of such risks as contracting HIV/AIDS or other sexually transmitted diseases, as well as smoking and driving while under the influence of alcohol or other drugs. In addition, more attention must be paid to teen adult communication throughout adolescence. Building on the lessons learned thus far, our ongoing project in other rural areas of New York focuses on this important protective factor, especially as it applies to rural youth.

KEY FINDINGS

- PDR/RDS techniques are successful in stimulating the participation of adolescents in risk prevention programs in rural areas.
- Rural teens are best reached by interventions located in their own communities.
- Teenagers with low HIV/AIDS knowledge scores were more likely to interact and recruit other teens with low knowledge levels than more knowledgeable youth.
- Participants regarded the peer-led educational intervention as highly valuable.
- Increased knowledge levels and decreased worry levels were observed at follow-up.
- At follow-up, 16- and 17-year-old participants reported higher rates of abstention from sex and 18 year olds reported higher rates of condom use than was found in YRBS data for the same year and age groups.

References

Annan, K. 2004. Statement of the Secretary General of the United Nations. Keynote address to the annual gala event of the International Women's Health Coalition, New York, January 15.

Berry, D.E. 2000. Rural acquired immunodeficiency syndrome in low and high prevalence areas. *South Med J.* 93(1): 36–43.

Bhattarai, Bidya. 2008. Safe motherhood in the context of Nepal. *Marriage and Family Review* 44 (2-3): 318–328.

Bianchi, A, D. Bishara, P. Enekwe, B. Frost, A. Kastning, J. Tiffany and S. Young. 2003. Friends inviting friends: Participant-driven recruitment in an HIV prevention research project. *Community Youth Development Journal* 4(1): 26–31.

Coale, Ansley J., and Judith Banister. 1996. Five decades of missing females in China. *Proceedings of the American Philosophical Society* 140: 421–450, December 4.

Conly, S.R., and S.L. Camp. 1992. *India's family planning challenges: From rhetoric to action.* Washington, DC: PCC.

Daniel, Elizabeth. 2009. Impact of psychological disorders in postpartum mothers and child: current issue in remediation in India. In Barbara, Wejnert, Nirupama Prakash, and Sue Steinmetz.(eds.). 2009. *Safe motherhood in a globalized world*. London: Routledge.

Glynn, M., and P. Rhodes. 2005. Estimated HIV prevalence in the United States at the end of 2003. National HIV Prevention Conference, June 2005, Atlanta, Georgia. Abstract 595.

Heckathorn, D., R. Broadhead, D. Weakliem, D. Anthony, H. Madray, R. Mills, and J. Hughes. 1998. Harnessing peer networks as an instrument for AIDS prevention: Results from a peer-driven intervention. *Public Health Reports*, supplement.

Koop Everett, Clarence Pearson and Roy Schwarz. 2002). *Critical issues in global health*. San Francisco, CA: Wiley Press.

Krauss, B.J., J. Tiffany, and L. Goldsamt. 1997. Research notes: Parent and pre-adolescent training for HIV prevention in a high seroprevalence neighbourhood. *AIDS/STD Health Promotion Exchange* 1: 10–12.

Kusi-Appouh, D. 2006. *Adolescent social networks: Knowledge, worry and risk/protective behaviors in rural New York*. Ithaca, NY: Cornell University.

Lewin, J.A., R. Weisell, S. Chevassus, C. Martinez, B. Burlingame, and A. Coward. 2001. The work burden of women. *Science* 294: 812–813.

Lo, Marieme. 2008. Public-private partnership for maternal health in Africa: Challenges and prospects. *Marriage and Family Review*, Vol. 2–3: 214–237.

Morgan, R. 1984. *Sisterhood is global*. New York: Anchors Books.

National AIDS Policy. 1996. Aids action plan. President Clinton announces a new strategy to reduce the impact of AIDS virus. PBS news online. Retrieved on March 1, 2008 at www.pbs.org/newshour/bb/health/.../**aids**_12-17.html

Parrott, Andrea and Nancy Cumming. 2008. *Sexual enslavement of girls and women worldwide*. London: Praeger.

Prakash, Nirupama. 2009. Training camp on safe motherhood in rural India: A research note. In Barbara, Wejnert, Nirupama Prakash, and Sue Steinmetz.(eds.). 2009. *Safe motherhood in a globalized world.* London: Routledge.

Romaniuk, Lara. 2002. A country in transition: Health crisis in Ukraine with focus on tobacco and alcohol. In B. Wejnert (ed.), *Transition to democracy in Eastern Europe and Russia*. Westport, CT: Praeger/Greenwood Press.

Sabu, George. 1997. Female infanticide in Tamil Nadu, India: from recognition back to denial? *Reproductive-Health-Matters*, pp. 124–132.

Salganik, Matthew J., and Douglas D. Heckathorn. 2004. Sampling and estimation in hidden populations using respondent-driven sampling. *Sociological Methodology*.

Singh, S., and J.E. Darroch. 2000. Adolescent pregnancy and childbearing: Levels and trends in developed countries. *Family Planning Perspectives* 32(1): 14–23.

Steinmetz, Suzanne. 2008. Challenges of safe motherhood: Program and policy recommendations. *Marriage and Family Review*, Vol. 2–3: 389–396.

Tiffany, J.S. 2006. Respondent-driven sampling in participatory research contexts: Participant-driven recruitment. *Journal of Urban Health*, Volume 83: 113–124.

United Nations. 2008. UN Web Services Section. Department of Public Information. Retrieved at www.un.org/millenniumgoals/.

Vijaykumar, Santosh. 2008. Communicating safe motherhood: Strategic messaging in a globalized world. *Marriage and Family Review*, Vol. 2–3: 173–200.

Wejnert, Barbara. 2003. The effects of growth of democracy and transition to market-based economies on women's well-being. *Journal of Consumer Policy* 26: 465–493.

Wejnert, Barbara, Nirupama Prakash, and Sue Steinmetz. (eds.) 2009. *Safe mother-hood in a globalized world.* London: Routledge.

World Health Organization. 2006. *Monitoring and evaluation.* Department of Re-productive Health and Research (RHR). Retrieved on May 12, 2009, at from http://www.who.int/reproductive_indicators/countrydata.asp ?page=1.

Name_____

Test Your Knowledge: Chapter 7

Short Answer Question

1. Describe the impact of science and technology on women's health. Provide at least three examples.

2. Can science and technology be used to empower women's health in the United States? And why?

3. Can science and technology be used to empower women and their health in underdeveloped countries? Provide a minimum of 3 examples.

Gender within the Global Development

Although the terms *globalization* and *global development* are frequently used together, there is a noteworthy distinction between the two.

The Concept of Globalization

The term *globalization* is recently understood as a process of economic, political, cultural and informational exchanges bonding local countries within the global world in which economy, and political and cultural systems are uniformly structured. As is understood there are positive and negative outcomes of globalization processes. "This requires articulation of the contradictions and ambiguities that globalization both is impose from above and yet can be contested and reconfigured from below...a view that theorizes globalization as highly complex, contradictory, and thus ambiguous set of institutions and social relations . . . " (Kellner 2002)

Initially, however, *globalization* was interpreted only in economic terms as one, joint capitalistic system that was broadly criticized. Accordingly globalization related to the development of an increasingly integrated global economy, marked by global trade, free flow of generated profit and capital across international borders, and the tapping of cheaper foreign labor markets. It was characterized by free access to markets; free access to information, including market information; the inability of firms to distort markets through government-imposed monopoly or oligopoly power; free movement of labor force between and within countries; and free movement of capital between and within countries.

In this context, the definition of globalization could be summarized as a free trade that refers to a trade based on the unrestricted international exchange of goods with tariffs used only as a source of revenue generated by involved in trade companies and institutions. Such trade allows bigger companies to internationally produce, compete, and maintain on the market the best quality products at inexpensive prices. Free trade greatly benefits large, multinational companies that succeed by saving on taxation and benefiting from unrestricted by tariffs trade. Consequently, the profit and revenues of large companies was speedily surpassing revenues of local businesses which, without the help of national governments through implementation of tariffs and tax relieve, was unprotected from aggressive competition, lowered prices, and economic fluctuations on the financial market. Unable to compete in selling quality goods for low prices locally, national businesses received little to no profit and were forced to bankruptcy.

Among other negative consequences were sweatshop production, overuse of land resources by foreign investors, lack of respect for workers rights and lack of concern for environmental protection by foreign industry). Globalization was also criticized for depriving states their individual entities and decision making power regarding own development. Only since the early 2000s, it has become clear, that the state is a more forceful and complex determinant of societal development than the literature on globalization would have predicted.

The Concept of Global Development

With the last decades, the meaning of globalization was broaden to incorporate the processes formerly known as *global development* which pertained to the broad scope of issues that affect societal life and were faced by societies and countries across the globe. These issues included capital flow, environmental concerns, economic growth, education, governance and democracy, international financial institutions and finances, food and agriculture, trade and development, global health policy, global market economy, inequality, migration and development, private investment, and security and peaceful initiatives.

Each issue was surrounded by a specific field of interests, characterized by a distinct set of parts and expectations. For example, in the case of governance and democracy, strong international institutions set the context for effective governance and were the key to generating development. Within this context, the decentralization of national governments took place and international governing institutions replaced weakening political authorities.

Similar processes took place within economic structures where national economies lost authority and were replaced by international agencies and economic institutions. Multinational companies and institutions guided the implementation of internationally developed initiatives. Consequently, many non-governmental, transnational organizations were established to fulfill the new demands and needs of citizens.

Under these conditions, a visible connection of local and global economy with local and global governance was established. In a speech given on April 22, 2002, U.S. President George W. Bush said, "Trade creates the habits of freedom, and those habits begin to create the expectations of democracy and demands for better democratic institutions. Societies that are open to commerce across their borders are more open to democracy within their borders" (Griswold 2006).

Global development or globalization in today's meaning, led to a softening of local boundaries and integration of regions. It limited territorial attachment and weakened the impact of the governing of independent states on matters of each country concerns. Simultaneously, concerns of each country became world concerns, as the interest of each country overlapped with the interest of other countries, and as the problem of each country affected countries globally.

Among other positive outcomes of contemporary globalization was provided education for citizens' of countries that were part of the globalized economic system, e.g. offered on job training of workers as foreign investors upgraded skills of employed workers, facilitated spread of educational exchanges, cross-border research collaboration, and joint educational initiatives. With opened international companies, new technology to host countries was transferred advancing less advanced states. Workers and professionals direct benefited gaining education and more skills.

The final positive outcome was flourishing cross-world mobility, which was expressed by countries' migration from rural to urban environments, as well as an international migration from underdeveloped to economically well-developed states. The mobility was stimulated by the intensified public demand for a higher standard of living, greater selection, and better and more consumer goods and services. Increasing mobility led to expansion of world tourism and transit of people. Under such circumstances, a demand for efficient transportation technologies advanced the development of new forms and means of transportation and communication, further bonding the world connectedness.

Rosenau (2003) observed that the global world joins the local worlds, creating one society of common concerns, overlapping economies, and interconnected governing. International communication, information technology, and mass transportation speed the link between global and local entities (see Figure 8.1).

Each society develops within the scope and in union with other developed and developing societies, as global development leads to the

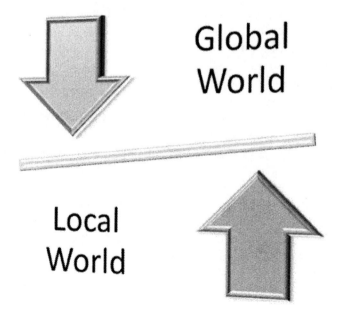

Figure 8.1 Interactive Equilibrium of the Local and Global World with Information Technology and Communication, Which Provide a Link Between the Global and Local Entities.

Source: Figure designed based on Rosenau's (2003) explanation of interactive influence of the global and local world.

Figure 8.2 International Training Workshop on Consultation and Experience Sharing on Issues of Management, Policy, and Other Concerns Pertinent to the Position of Women in a Developing World, Organized by the UNIFEM, United Nations, at Birla Institute of Technology in Pilani, India, on October 2006.

Source: Photo by Barbara Wejnert, taken during the United Nations workshop at Birla Institute of Technology, Pilani, Rajasthan, India.

intensive, dense, and rapid exchange of goods and symbols (e.g., McDonalization) on a planetary scale. Under such conditions, human interactions are disembodied from their local context.

The current challenge of global development is to focus on how policies of the developed world can be better targeted toward strengthening governance systems, economic progress, and societal support in developing countries through avenues of intervention such as foreign aid and trade policy; and training workshops, consultation, and experience sharing on issues of management, policy, and other concerns pertinent to the developing world (see Figure 8.2).

Among today's global problems are the international costs of state failure, the risks of climate change, cross-border corruption, sex and drug trafficking, the missing Green Revolution in Africa, and the slow pace of international action to reduce world poverty. Each of these problems points to the potential benefits of more effective and more legitimate global institutions. Thus, there is an increasing recognition that global markets require good global politics. Good global politics are critical to the battle against global poverty and unrealized human development, and to a more just and fair as well as a more stable and prosperous global economy.

A common belief, hence, is that globalization of markets can and has brought mutual benefits to both the rich and the poor. Yet, there is contention over how these benefits are divided. The world's poorest countries, in sub-Saharan Africa and elsewhere, are growing slowly, and the gap between the richest and poorest countries is widening. Inequality within many countries is also increasing. The world is not uniform; inequality and injustice in the global economy demonstrates the inherent asymmetries of a developing world. Throughout the developing world, contrasting pictures of modern and outdated poverty existence are commonly visible.

Globalization and free trade leads to benefits but also many disadvantages. Globalization as a continuation of market capitalism fails to note, as some argue, that new forms and modes of capitalism developed due to the new technologies, and economic methods do not benefit equally all strata within societies or all countries. Because large multinational companies are developed based on financial and management support from prominent well-developed countries, globalization mainly benefits the well-developed core countries, further enhancing and strengthening their economic position in the world system (Wallerstein 2002).

Contrasting this argument are opinions that the least-developed states gain from the globalization of markets as much as the most-developed states, whereas the semi-developed "middle-level economies" are among the losers (Garrett 2004). The distribution of foreign direct investment (FDI) in developing countries is rarely in services in which the labor force of the middle economies are trained; hence, no benefits are gained in countries with a middle-level economy (Shafer 1994).

As the world stands today, there are many countries that are economically unable to benefit from globalization and free trade. The absence of trade-distorting policies (e.g., taxes, subsidies for local producers, tariffs, trade barriers like quotas on imports) that give small firms, local businesses, and households an advantage over multinational corporations deters prosperity in developing countries. Poorer countries need to tax multinational companies to develop themselves. Luck of control over the trade and a tax break add to greater asymmetry in the world's economic development.

The Golden Arches, the familiar trademark of McDonald's restaurants, symbolically superimposed over the global development, is a sign of success of globalization. As it is believed, a country with McDonald's (and hence an accepting global market economy) will not be involved in war because the country is economically stable enough to support international chains and has no need to invade elsewhere for resources. Mutual interconnectedness stimulated by trade would strengthen international relations and spread democratic governing, leading to diffusion of modern technology, science, and education (Watson 2006). Countries will compete for better products—not for resources—which will prevent conflict and foster further development.

Thus, global and local politics that aim at mutual benefit of the local and global world are critical to prosperous global development, where the positives and negatives outcomes of globalization weigh each other out.

Global Development/Globalization and Women

Position of Women Before the Period of Global Development

Prior to the period of global development, the statistics for gender equality were grim. With two-thirds of the world's illiterate being women and overall women illiteracy rate increasing in contrast to the decreasing illiteracy globally. In addition, one-third of all the world's families are single families headed by women. Nonetheless, women own less than 1 percent of the world's property, contribute to two-thirds of all working hours, and in developed countries earn 50 to 75 percent of what men earn. In the developing world, women produce more than 50 percent of all the food supply (in most African countries, more than 90 percent) and do 60 to 80 percent of all agricultural work in the world. But out of 500 million people who suffer from hunger and malnutrition, most of them are women and children under 5 years of age. Of the 22 million people who die yearly from starvation, most of them are women and children.

Such a situation stimulated the interest of international agencies and organization, and equality of women in developing world became a topic at meetings of international forums. "While women represent half of the global population and one-third of the labor force, they receive only one-tenth of the world income and own less than one percent of world property. They also are responsible for two-thirds of all working hours" pronounced the Kurt Waldheim, Secretary of the United Nations of 1972-1977 (Morgan 1984).

Some have argued that a necessary step toward gender equality is global economic development and industrialization, which, by stimulating job growth, can facilitate women's access to wage income, better education, provision of health-care, and empowerment of women's position within families as well as local and national decision-making institutions. Though it appears, intuitively, that economic development fosters economic opportunities, a causal link between gender equality and economic development is not unquestionable.

Position of Women Since the Period of Global Development

Global development has been associated with the massive expansion in the informal sector. Most women from the developing world are engaged in work in the booming informal sector of unpaid or underpaid domestic labor, which is increasing due to limitation of social welfare in the capitalistic system.

Women from developing countries are also involved in the outsourced production link to industrial sector produced outside traditional work places. The new informal economy "responds quickly to changes in the economic and institutional environment and adapts to enveloping patterns of work organization in the more formal sector, taking up the gaps that it leaves behind" (Beneria 2003, 3).

Evidence from fast-developing and underdeveloped countries, however, leaves in question whether the process of economic development can guarantee an improvement in women's relative status. Globalization has brought about advances in education and more gender parity in wages for a limited number of women in the formal economy. However, global, sustained economic growth and industrialization over the past 25 years has not resulted in a significant reduction of the gender wage gap. The new technologies are only a part of global restructuring and are not autonomous forces that are changing societies and break prior forms of social organization.

Despite several decades of built awareness of gender inequality, undertaken by the United Nations Fourth World Conference on Women in Beijing, China, in 1995, followed by the conference at Beijing in 2005, and Millennium Development Goals of the United Nations, gender inequality remains prevalent throughout the world. Even in advanced industrial nations, the women's share of the labor force is lower and their unemployment rate is higher than men's, professional advancement is deterred, and female involvement in housework is disproportionate compared to male counterparts.

Young women in developing countries are relied on to provide cheap, educated labor to the dominant labor-intensive export industries (electronics, textiles and clothing). National governments facilitate this process through the expansion of educational opportunities and programs to increase the labor force participation rates of single and married women. The need for an inexpensive, qualified labor force is visible especially during the early phase of merging within a global market, when the shift from a concentration on extraction and export of raw materials and on agricultural production to the production of manufactured goods and the growth of service sectors takes place.

In this early stage of a global development, national economic strategies of import-substitution, which favored the production of intermediate-level capital goods and consumer products for home markets, replace strategies that favor the production of goods for export to world market (Moghadam 2000). With acceptance of the global market economy, the state's primary goal of attaining export-driven growth has been supported by policies to make exports available to a world market at an attractive price (Seguino 1997). Particularly, some newly industrialized countries (NICs) that experienced the transition from agricultural and low-income countries to industrialize and upper middle-income countries, experience increasing women labor force participation mainly in low-paying jobs.

Women Empowerment as a Turning Point in the Global Development

In what sense are global development and gender interconnected? Is women's empowerment important and, if yes, why is it so important?

To summarize the work of many scholars and institutions, the general claim is that empowerment of women is critical to global development and democracy. The recent Millennium Development Goals expresses this claim within the initiatives of the Asian Development Bank, the World Bank, and USAID, and is part of an agenda of the United States foreign policy. The understanding of women empowerment is incorporated within the objectives of the United Nations initiatives since 1984. Why is this issue imperative to modern development?

A comparative study of women's earned income conducted in Bangladesh, Brazil, Canada, Ethiopia, and Great Britain revealed that higher women's income led to an increase of child survival rates by 20 times and an improvement of child weight-height indicator by 8 times. As was rationalized, women devote their earnings to provide for the family, especially for health care and the nutritional needs of young children, which overwhelmingly reduces young child mortality and health.

Interesting, an increase of men's income did not lead to as high results, mostly because the priority in men's provision is in macro-structures of family existence such as housing, family transportation, or domestic production (Coleman 2004).

Equally beneficial for societal well-being is women's education. According to some studies, an increase of education of girls lowered birth rates more than heavily advertised family planning. Longer education not only increases women's earning capacity, but also prevents child-marriage of teenage daughters.

A study by Nobel Laureate Muhammad Yunus, economist, developer of micro-lending, and author of *Banker to the Poor*, argued that women's borrowing when using microcredit not only increased their earning abilities, but also increased their involvement in the family decision-making process and increased the family social mobility due to an accumulation of wealth. Women having increased status within families and community are more involved in political processes and aware of legal, health, and family services available to women and families. Their empowerment eventually decreases domestic violence (see Figure 8.3). *Microcredit* (micro-lending) is defined as the extension of very small loans to those in poverty, designed to spur entrepreneurship. The initial capital is generated by voluntary contribution of monthly saving by members of a small group. The capital is distributed to borrowers, who by paying it back provide capital for distribution in the form of a loan to the next member of the group. The users of micro-lending are mainly women who lack collateral, steady employment and a verifiable credit history, and therefore cannot meet even the most minimal qualifications to gain receive any traditional bank credit.

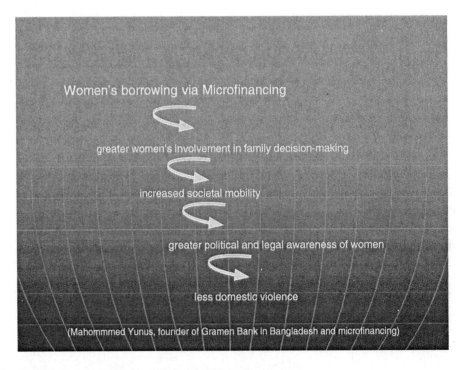

Figure 8.3 Summary of Results of Muhammad Yunus Studies.

Source: Figure created by the author, based on the results of Muhammad Yunus studies.

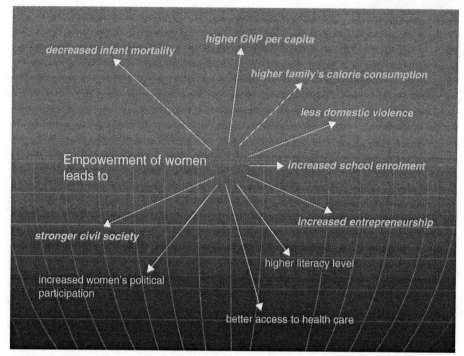

Figure 8.4 Outcomes of Women Empowerment.

Source: Figure created by the author, based on literary sources addressing women empowerment (e.g., Beneria 2003, Coleman 2004, Wejnert, Steinmetz, and Prakash 2009).

Other scholars indicated the benefits of empowerment of women as it increases the level of societal education, improves health, decrease violence, and enhances economic and political development (see Figure 8.4).

References

Beneria, L. 2003. *Gender, development, and globalization: Economics as if all people mattered.* London: Routledge.

Bush, George W. (January 2001.) *Rallying the Armies of Compassion.* White House Press Release.

Coleman, Isabel. 2004. The payoff from women's rights. *Foreign Affairs,* review paper, May/June: 79-94.

Garrett, Geofrey. (2000). "The causes of Globalization." *Comparative Political Studies* 33; 941-991.

Griswold, Daniel. 2006. Using globalization to spread democracy around the world. In John Balonze (ed.), *Debating globalization.* Paris: GYAN France.

Kellner, Douglass. 2002. Theorizing Globalization. *Sociological Theory,* 20 (3): 285-305.

Moghadam, V.M. 2000. Gender and the global economy. In M.M. Ferree, J. Lorber, and B.B. Hess (eds.), *Revisioning gender.* Lanham, MD: Rowman & Littlefield.

Morgan, R. 1984. *Sisterhood is global.* New York: Anchors Books.

Muhammad, Yunus. 2003. *Banker to the poor. Micro-lending and the battle against world poverty.* Canada: Public Affairs Inc.

Rosenau, J. 2003. *Distant proximities: dynamics beyond globalization.* Princeton, NJ: Princeton University Press.

Seguino, S. 1997. Export-led growth and persistence of gender inequality in the newly industrialized countries. In J. M. Rives and M. Yousefi (eds.), *Economic dimensions of gender inequality: A global perspective.* Westport, CT: Praeger.

Shafer, W. 1994. *Winners and Loosers*. Ithaca, NY: Cornell University Press.

Wallerstein, Immanual. 2002. Democracy, Capitalism, and Transformation. In O. Enwezor. et al. (Eds.) *Democracy unrealized*. Documenta 11-Platform 1. Ostfildern—Ruit: Hatje Cantz, 96-110.

Waston, James. 2006. *Golden arches east*. Palo Alto, CA: Stanford University Press.

Wejnert, Steinmetz, and Prakash. 2009. Conceptual Framework for Integrating Perspectives and Approaches to Problems of Safe Motherhood. In B. Wejnert, S. Steinmentz & N. Prakash (Eds.) *Safe motherhood in globalized world*. London: Routledge Press: 2–13.

Name_____

Test Your Knowledge: Chapter 8

Short Answer Questions

1. Compare and define the terms global development and globalization.

2. Define and explain the main components of globalization.

3. In what way does globalization affect the states of women. Provide the positive and negative effects of globalization.

The Impact of Global Development on Gender: Lessons to Be Learned

Four important lessons can be learned from the interchange between gender and global development. First, in contrast to most analyses focusing on economy and politics in a global context (e.g., Kentor and Boswell 2003, Sonntag 2004, A.T. Kearny 2001), global development does not take place in political and economic vacuums, but occurs simultaneously in all major spheres of societal life. It effects essential institutions, from government and economic institutions, to cultural customs and norms. The interconnectedness of basic social institutions leads to multifocal effects and challenges to women's empowerment, as indicated throughout this book (see Figure 9.1).

Second, a major lesson is understanding that global development is a process that did not start with the 1970–1980s era of globalization but long before that time. This process is rooted and affected by historical events of economic and political domination; colonization; bias cultural superiority of the Western countries that lead to division of the world on faster and slower developing South and North; wealthy and poor societies; independent and dependent economies; and core, semi-peripheries, and peripheries. Included in this volume chapters on feminist ideology and feminist movement; macro-perspective on gender; global violence, women and work, global health, and global development and gender; illustrate that such world division has not only a long-term impact on the current development of countries, but also on opportunities open to women globally. Gender discrimination in salaries, women's unpaid work, the undervaluing of the social position of women, insufficient provision for nutritional needs leading to poor health, inadequate provision of health care, and prevalent mistreatment of women were expressed well before the time of the diffusing global economy and unequal societal development. The coming era of global development should thus constitute the long-awaited time of eliminating the difficulties that women are faced with every day.

Third, this book provides a lesson in understanding the impact of a global development on gender, a process that not only stems from politics and economy, but also is rooted in traditional customs, stereotypes, beliefs, and practices that have dominated societal life throughout history. Presented perspectives on the inequality of women and strategies undertaken by the feminist movement reflect the multilevel, complex processes of gender bias in organizations of societies. A transition from gender-unequal to gender-equal society is achievable with joint efforts of feminist organizations and supportive social policies developed during worldwide global development. The author purposely selected themes of gender inequality such as health, work, education, professional advancement, and traditionalism of gender roles to provide the broadest and most comprehensive knowledge about the extent of the disadvantage position of women across the world. The detailed illustrations of problems that women encounter daily address the need to empower women. Women empowerment could be seen as a vehicle for the implementation of change. This book can inform political advisors, policy makers, scholars, as well as a broader audience on the complex matter of global development and its impact on gender and women empowerment, transferring knowledge into practical policy solutions and interventions.

The final lesson is the comprehensive approach to knowledge about global development in terms of societal equity, utilization of existing human resources, increase of health, decrease of violence, and creation of societal wealth. Examining cross-world similarities of the devaluated position of women is a good starting point for global policy implementation and establishing universal laws that secure a just and prosperous development of mankind. Women empowerment within global development could lead to an overall increase of societal wealth, security, civil participation, and democratic governing. Moreover, women empowerment is also essential to the prosperity of future generations because mothers' well-being and their children well-being are inseparable.

References

Kearny, A.T. 2001. Measuring globalization. Carnegie Endowment for International Peace. *Foreign Policy*, January/February.

Kentor, Jeffrey, and Terry Boswell. 2003. Foreign capital dependence and development: A new direction. *American Sociological Review* 68: 2.

Sonntag, Heinz. 2004. Globalization and democracy. An interview with Fernando Henrique Cardoso. *Political Sociology Newsletter*, American Sociological Association.

EMPOWERED OF WOMEN AND SOCIETIES

- Increase social status of women
- Increase occupational opportunities for women
- Increase in women participation in science, politics and management
- Increase use of women abilities
- Increase women and mothers' health
- Increase children health and mobility
- Reduce gender discriminatory customs
- Increase societal wealth
- Increase societal health
- Increase societal literacy and education
- Increase of human resources and potential
- Reduced societal violence
- More just societies
- Increase civil participation

PROGRAM AND POLICY INTERVENTIONS

- Work toward the goal of universal primary school
- Provide mechanisms to reduce extreme poverty
- Provide programs to reduce malnutrition and starvation
- Develop programs and policies to increase the value of females
- Develop programs to increase self-sufficiency
- Increase availability of nutritional supplements
- Provide programs to increase women entrepreneurship
- Provide ICT tools to increase knowledge and resources available to women
- Provide awareness of spread of gender violence
- Outlaw violence against women
- Encourage grass-roots involvement in all programs
- Spread knowledge about women health
- Provide employment to women
- Provide materials that are cultural- and language-specific
- Outlaw underpaid female labor
- Provide programs to reduce feminization of poverty

SOCIETAL CHALLENGES

- Extreme poverty
- Food insufficiency
- Lack of technology
- Resources insufficiency
- Low levels of literacy
- Lack of education
- Underrepresentation in science
- Underrepresentation in managerial, political, and technological fields

GENDER-RELATED CHALLENGES

- Low status relative to males
- Women devalued
- Lower levels of literacy
- Lack of formal education
- Lack of knowledge and access to modern technology
- Inadequate general health care
- Low social position in families
- Control and isolation of women
- Discriminatory gender roles

CULTURAL CHALLENGES

- Traditional Customs
- Cultural norms of maleness
- Cultural models of womanhood
- Gender stereotypes
- Media image of gender
- Misunderstanding of feminism goals

Figure 9.1. An Impact of Global Development on Gender Equality: Challenges and Policy Interventions

Test Your Knowledge: Final Examination

Research Paper Guidelines

Instructions: Choose one of the described topics.

The research paper needs to focus on one of the international gender topics in the syllabus of the course. The outline of the paper and its title needs to be approved by the course instructor by April 15. For the research paper, you will need to select either (1) a policy program, (2) an organization's program, or (3) a socio-economic trend that most likely, in your opinion, will have predictable impact on either (1) gender relations or gender roles or both in society, or (b) individual citizens' (men and/or women) well-being. Trace this impact from a logical starting point to an end point (the latter may be arbitrarily set), thinking about yourself as a primary government member, influential policy maker, government adviser, or activist in a gender-oriented movement or organization.

> *Example 1:* Since the beginning of the 1980s, the rapid growth of globalization in the world is believed to correlate with the American dream of equal and open opportunities for citizens of all countries.

> *Example 2:* Because of global development, waves of immigrants have come to the United States, bringing their cultural norms and values including standards for gender roles. With the adjustment to American culture, their gender norms have changed, which some might believe are symbols of lost cultural identity. Take one of two opposite stances and discuss how the identity can be preserved or how American culture can impose greater gender assimilation.

Brainstorm about all of the possible effects of this policy, law, or trend. It will help you to distinguish between direct and indirect effects. Also, pay attention to the level at which gender relations or the individual is affected. Are gender relations and individuals affected by a change in cultural values in the society as a whole? Are there any changes in each gender's or individual's resources (time, money, food) or needs (number of children, need for professional help). It may be some combination of these, or a change in one may lead to changes in others.

After you have generated several ideas, try to organize them in a causal chain, explaining what leads to what and how each thing is connected to others.

> *Example 1:* Since the beginning of the 1990s, the world is rapidly globalizing, including underdeveloped states.

DIRECT EFFECT	INDIRECT EFFECT
• Development of market economy	• Greater societal awareness of competition so better quality products
• Change in labor market across the world (due to outsourcing, low skill labor force)	
	• Reduction of jobs for women in some countries and feminization of labor in other countries
	• Feminization of poverty
• Lower status of women	• Decline of women's well-being

Finally, think about possible interventions that could change what you have predicted, and design hypothetical policies that you would like to implement to make the transition toward more equal gender relations smoother and more just.

The paper should not exceed 10 pages, not including references.